THE WELL
Overflows

From My Heart to Yours
Timeless Truths in a Global Crisis

John Flanner MBE

Published by John Flanner MBE 2020
email: john@flanner.co.uk
website: www.johnflanner.co.uk
John Flanner can also be found on LinkedIn and Facebook

Printed by Pendlee Print 2020

Copyright John Flanner 2020

The right of John Flanner to be identified as the author of this work has been asserted in accordance with sections 77 and 78 of the Copyright, Designs and Patents Act 1988.

A catalogue record for this book is available from the British Library.

ISBN 978-0-9934175-8-0

All rights reserved. No part of this publication may be reproduced, stored in a retrieval system or transmitted in any form or by any means, electronic, mechanical, photocopying, recording, or otherwise, without the prior permission of the publishers.

Typeset in 12pt Calibri

Cover design by Elizabeth Webb

Genre: Christian/Inspirational

Contents

Dedication

Foreword

Introduction

Articles

1. Alive and Kicking!
2. Angels on Assignment
3. Around the World in 26 Days
4. Bars and Stars
5. Big Doors Swing on Small Hinges (Part 1)
6. Big Doors Swing on Small Hinges (part 2)
7. Bite It and Believe It
8. Black is Black
9. Can I Be "Selfish" and Expect God to Bless Me?
10. Caterpillars and Butterflies
11. Donkey Ride, Anyone?
12. Excite God!
13. Football and Heaven
14. Getting to Know You
15. God Knows What He's Doing
16. Guide Dog to Guide God
17. Guard God
18. High-Rise Howlers
19. Honour God and One Another
20. How to Flow in the Purposes of God
21. Hypocrite (Part 1)
22. Hypocrite (Part 2)
23. "Jesus, Jesus, Jesus!"
24. Jesus the Super-Sub
25. Keep on Drinking
26. Keep the Home Fire Burning!

27. Launch Out into the Deep (Part 1)
28. Launch Out into the Deep (Part 2)
29. Local Church - The Benefits of Belonging
30. My Father Loves Me
31. My First Answered Prayer
32. My Heart Overflows (Psalm 45:1)
33. No More Sad Songs
34. O What a Night!
35. On My Knees
36. School Reports
37. Seven Up!
38. Silver Linings
39. Sing and Dance!
40. Stand Up and Live – The Choice is Yours
41. Take Your Harp Down from the Willow Tree
42. Taste and See!
43. The Birds are Singing!
44. The Credibility Gap
45. The Greatest Discovery
46. Tributes Come Pouring In
47. Wanted Dead or Alive
48. Was Blind but Now I See!
49. Way Back into Love
50. Weapons of Mass Destruction
51. What's Your Hallelujah Like?
52. When Johnny Cash Sang
53. Worriers or Warriors?
54. Your Move!

Appendix – Poems, Prayers and Promises

Acknowledgments

Other Books by the Same Author

"From My Heart to Yours"

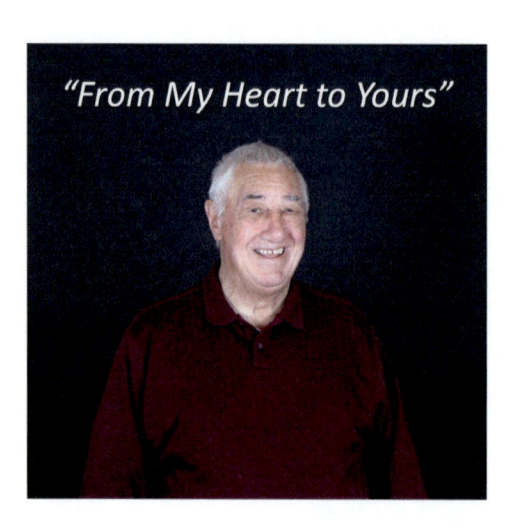

Dedication

This book is dedicated to the memory of my beloved wife, Sylvia, who went to be with Jesus, two days after our 49th wedding anniversary. She features in several of the stories contained in its pages.

As a family, we decided it would be a fitting tribute to donate a memorial bench to Elmdon Park, Solihull, one of Sylvia's favourite parks. It's a lovely location and near to where Sylvia used to take the children to picnic and play.

The wording on the bench reads:

In Loving Memory of Sylvia Rose Flanner
(8 January 1950 – 1 December 2018)
Greatly missed by all family and friends
You brought joy and laughter to so many –
Now lighting up Heaven with your smile

I pray this book will light up your life, provide you with a few smiles along the way, and greatly inspire you to move into God's purposes for you.

John Flanner MBE

Foreword

John Flanner is a natural communicator. I first heard him speak to a class of children, regaling them with stories of living without sight: about falling down a workman's hole; stepping off the last carriage of a train which hadn't pulled far enough along the platform; his braille-pecking budgie; and the fun to be had with a white stick. You could hear a pin drop!

I later invited John to be the guest speaker for some over-60s and I realized that he seemed to have a sixth sense about what his audience needed to hear. His place of employment also picked up on that ability to communicate, and he was commissioned to address and inspire work colleagues. With his disarming honesty, hallmark humour and positivity, he would deliver his talks … and a motivational speaker was born.

Also a gifted writer, John recorded his much-loved stories in an autobiography, *Fear Fun and Faith*. Two other books followed suit, and now, a fourth has been added!

"THE WELL *Overflows*" was born out of the 2020 Coronavirus pandemic when the world went into lockdown. John's isolation was stricter that most, but he chose to turn a *problem* into a *possibility* and started to write a few articles, initially for Facebook readers. These soon began to appear daily and it seemed that fresh waters from The Well (the affectionate name for John's apartment) went into full flow. You can now enjoy the whole collection all in one book! It is interesting to think of other books which came out of lockdown situations. Not least the famous letters of St Paul and John Bunyan's, Pilgrims Progress.

John's zeal for life is infectious. He wholeheartedly believes that this springs from a life-changing encounter with Jesus Christ. His passion and purpose is to share that same abundant life with all he meets. This book is another expression of that.

As you read through each article – perhaps one a day – you too can draw from that same well which sustains John.

Jesus said to the woman at the well: *" ... whoever drinks the water I give them will never thirst again." John 4:14*

Drink ... and be satisfied!

Elizabeth Webb – a family friend
July 2020

Introduction

In February of 2019, just over two months after my wife of 49 years had died, I made the bold (some would say reckless) decision to sell up the family home of 29 years and move into a two bedroom assisted-living apartment. I did not plan this in advance. When the email invitation dropped into my inbox, I actually thought it was junk mail and hastily deleted it.

As the day progressed, however, I had a nagging feeling that I should have read that email. I returned to my computer and retrieved it from my deleted items and, using my JAWS screen-reading software, began to read it.

It transpired that I was being invited to view a property that had unexpectedly become available. It sounded ideal, so I arranged an appointment and went to look at it with two of my daughters. It was amazing and I knew instantly this was the right place for me. As someone who had been blind since the age of 19, my culinary skills were more-or-less non-existent, stretching only to making toast or microwave meals. With this new place being assisted living, it meant that all my meals would be provided. The children would not be concerned about me; I would be fed and live in a safe environment.

I am so happy here and thank God every day for providing this wonderful place for me to live. Very early on in my new home, I began to feel this was a place of great refreshing, providing the perfect opportunity for me to come to terms with the loss of Sylvia. One of my daughters placed photographs of Sylvia and the family around the place, so helping make it really homely.

While praising God one morning, I had the sense that the apartment was like a well out of which was flowing streams of living water. I decided I was going to prophetically call my apartment "The Well".
For Father's Day in 2019 one of my daughters gave me a plaque on which was engraved the words "The Well" and so it was placed

prominently on my front door. Now to family, friends and folk who work here, my apartment is known to them all as "The Well".

As we approached lockdown because of the coronavirus pandemic, I was challenged by a friend to consider writing a regular inspirational piece to go on my Facebook page. Knowing that without sight I am not able to navigate Facebook very well, she offered to upload articles for me and give me feedback on any responses.

Not one to shirk a challenge, I decided to prayerfully "give it a go". The result is that I have written over 50 articles, which have yielded an encouraging response. Several people felt these postings, which have a short shelf-life on Facebook, were worthy of being put into a book so they could inspire and encourage more people.

With that endorsement ringing in my ears, I went to work on putting the book together and the result is what you are reading now! Many of the articles you will read reflect and capture a particular time in history, yet its messages are timeless and eternal.

During the three months of lockdown, the phrase "From My Home to Yours" has been used repeatedly by broadcasters and church leaders. I've slightly adapted that to say that this book truly comes with love "From My Heart to Yours" and I pray that the well of living water will continue to overflow into your life.

John Flanner MBE
July 2020

1. ALIVE AND KICKING!

I awoke on the morning of Wednesday 8 January 2020 with no reason to believe this was going to be anything other than a routine kind of a day. How wrong I would find that to be as the morning unfolded.

Wednesday 8 January 2020 would, in fact, have been my wife Sylvia's 70th birthday had she not died some 13 months earlier.

Going about my usual early morning chores, I was alerted to a text message on my phone. On checking it, I discovered it was from my grandson Elliot to say that his girlfriend Imagen had gone into labour with their first child. An hour or so later, my excited grandson rang me with the news that Oscar had been born into the world and that mother and baby were doing well. Elliot was so excited, exclaiming "Grandad, I cannot believe Oscar has been born on Nan's 70th birthday".

I was thrilled about this because the happy event took my mind off Sylvia's death and birthday, on to the new life that had just been born.

I felt buoyant as I prepared myself to go off to a midweek service at my home church. The service was a good one and I was able to share my good news with quite a few people. As my friends drove me home and pulled up outside my apartment block, we were greeted by Allison, one of my daughters. Ally was clearly very excited saying, "Isn't it wonderful, Dad? Two babies on Mum's birthday".

"Why, I only know of one?" was my puzzled reply.

Ally then went on to explain that Amy, one of my granddaughters, had been rushed into hospital and given birth to Daisy some seven weeks early. I could hardly contain myself. To say this was amazing is an understatement. As I sat with my lunch, I was quietly pondering the events of the morning. Suddenly the phone began to ring. It was my daughter Beverley, one of the new grandmothers to baby Oscar. Bev was noticeably shaky and tearful as she blurted out "Dad, this is incredible, two babies on Mum's birthday, I can't believe it".

I quietly agreed saying, "It really is wonderful".

Bev continued, "I have to tell you Dad, a couple of weeks ago I was really missing Mum and could not stop crying so from deep inside I cried out, please Mum give me a sign that you are alive. What greater sign could I have than two babies on her birthday, one a little bit late and the other seven weeks early. I now know Mum is alive".

With that, the tears rolled down my face and into my soup, but I didn't care. Bev and I were shedding tears on either end of the phone.

The babies continue to do well but within the family none of us will ever forget Sylvia's 70th birthday even if she was not physically here to share it with us. Now we know she is where she said she would be, in Heaven safe in the presence of Jesus, her friend Saviour and Lord.

Surely both the babies, and Sylvia, are alive and kicking!

* * *

2. ANGELS ON ASSIGNMENT

In my 51 years as a Christian I have not read a book about Angels, apart from the Bible, that is. I have never been interested in angels (perhaps to my shame) and often viewed reported sightings of them with a large pinch of the proverbial salt. Though the Bible has a lot to say about angels they did not, as I thought, impact on my everyday life.

I do remember, however, being at a Bible Week in the Yorkshire Dales, which was very special, I have to say. One day, the local newspaper carried a front-page headline declaring that angels had been singing loudly and sweetly in the early hours of the morning inside the main arena. It was the only explanation that could be given after many reports of the singing coming from the Royal Agricultural Showground in Harrogate, where the event was being held. There were certainly no human beings in there at that time of the morning.

I have been at events where people have said angels have been present in the meeting and I know of reputable people who have claimed to have had an angelic visitation. For me, however, it is a subject that has never grabbed my attention, until now that is!

A dear friend enthused to me about a book he had read at least twice. It excited him so much that he said he would love to read it to me. "What's the title?" I asked.

"It's called Angels on Assignment and it's brilliant. I think you will love it," he said glowingly.

Whilst not at the time quite sharing his level of enthusiasm, I agreed to him reading it to me. Well I have to say it has blessed me beyond my wildest dreams, and I would like to share with you some of the things that have thrilled me. I can, in no way, do this book justice but if it whets your appetite, it is available free to read online or you can purchase a copy from Amazon.

Angels on Assignment by Roland Buck is the amazing account of a series of visitations that angels made to Roland at his home. (Just to say, Roland was no eccentric crackpot.) He was an established Pastor of an Assemblies of God church in America for nearly 40 years. When the angels came, Roland wrote down every message that they gave him and the only person he shared these things with initially, was his wife. At one point, Roland was given a list of 120 names of people, things and situations and the angel said these things would take place in the order that they were on the list over a two-year period. That is exactly what happened, and Roland describes several of these occurrences.

Roland describes how the Angel Gabriel came to see him quite often, accompanied at other times by Michael. He said they were perhaps seven feet tall and they were dressed in similar clothes to us, though Gabriel and Michael also wore gold sashes. Several other angels of lesser rank came too, and they all had names and were dressed in open neck shirts, normal trousers and shoes. He also commented that their hairstyles were similar to ours.

Roland goes on to say that there are worshipping angels, warring angels (of whom Michael is the Commander) and ministering angels whose job it is to watch over and minister to the likes of you and me.

At one point, Gabriel had to take his leave for a short time and leave Roland with the other angel, because he said the Lord required him. After a short time, he returned.

On one memorable occasion Gabriel said the Lord wanted to see Roland and so Gabriel took him to Heaven and, though he did not see the Lord's face, he had a conversation with him. Roland said the Lord showed him the vast room where all of the files of every person who has ever lived is kept. The Lord took out a few files of people we know from the Bible and then he took out Roland's file. He let Roland look at it and he looked with some trepidation. Roland, remembering some of the bad things he had done in his life, could not find them. When Roland asked why there was nothing bad on his file, the Lord said it was because they had all been blotted out by the blood of Jesus. What great news is that, then!

God also said to Roland that he did not want his people to fear Judgement Day. God said that, on that great day, it was his opportunity to give thanks to all his people for their devotion and works of service. If you are anything like me that is so reassuring because, at the back of my mind, there has been a little bit of a fear of Judgement Day.

When Roland returned from Heaven with the angels, he found that he had only been away from his house for a few minutes. Heaven is that close, and it gives weight to the Scripture, "Absent from the body, present with the Lord". Time and eternity are so incredibly different. This book certainly provides many insights into the eternal.

It is fascinating to read the part Gabriel played in the parting of the Red Sea and how the angels were present when the walls of Jericho came tumbling down.

One final thing from me. When we pray in accordance with God's will, our prayers are heard and the angels are sent out on assignment to bring that prayer to pass. This book has done me the power of good, reinvigorating my prayer life and made me so much aware of the myriads of angels who are on assignment every day.

* * *

3. AROUND THE WORLD IN 26 DAYS

Growing up I was very familiar with the phrase *Around the World in 80 Days*. It first came to my attention because I heard it on the wireless (doesn't that take you back?) as it was the title of a hit record by Bing Crosby. I later discovered that there was a film of the same name, starring English actor David Niven. Later on in my education, I became aware that Around the World in 80 Days was a novel, first published in the 1870s and written by the French author Jules Verne. A great adventure saga that is worth looking into.

I have never heard of the phrase, "Around the world in 26 days" though, so I think I can claim to have invented it! Let me explain...

I mention elsewhere that, while I was living in Cornwall attending a Bible College, I went to an early morning prayer meeting where we prayed for the nations. It was there I began to realise how much God loves the nations of the world and praying for them each day was so energizing. It certainly helped me and others to engage with the news a lot more and celebrate as we saw our prayers having a great effect.

This experience greatly influenced me, and I have continued to pray for the nations ever since, occasionally taking a short break so as to come back revived when I felt I was becoming stale.

John 3:16 "For God so loved the world, that he gave his only Son so that whoever believes in him will not perish, but have eternal life" is in itself enough to encourage us to pray for the world, In the Bible, God uses many phrases to express his love for all, such as *"all ethnic groups," "all nations," "all peoples," "all mankind," "all creation," "every creature," "every knee," "every tongue," "men of every language,"* and *"the world."*

It has been my experience that, as you pray for the nations of the world, we touch God's heart in a very special way. I once heard someone say that most Christians spend most of their lives praying on the postage stamp of their own miserable existence. Attention-grabbing or what? The speaker said that if you put a postage stamp on an envelope of whatever size and we limit ourselves to praying on the postage stamp, we are missing the rest of the envelope. Strange illustration I know, but I got the point and could identify with it.

There is a world out there to be won to Jesus and we need to shape up and get stuck in at whatever level we are at. God will honour us if we simply make a start.

You could start at the first day of the month. There are 26 letters in the alphabet, so begin praying for all of the countries you can think of beginning with the letter "A". You do not have to spend long on each one, but simply mentioning them before God is a start. I have been encouraged by the Apostle Paul because he writes, "I make mention of you in my prayers" and sometimes that is all we need to do. As you get more into it, then the Holy Spirit may lead you to pray more specifically for a certain nation, or people group.

This is an exercise in prayer more to be enjoyed than endured, though sometimes it may have to be the latter. It does not matter that you do not know of every nation on the planet, you are only accountable for what you do know. Of course, some letters have very few nations, whilst others have many, especially the letter "S". That does not matter. The most important thing at this stage is to get into the discipline of it and, as you grow in confidence, then you can become more creative and be led by the Holy Spirit.

I would point out that when you get to the letter "I", which could depict selfishness, look what nations you have: Ireland, Italy, Iran, Iraq, Israel, India, Indonesia, Ivory Coast and Iceland. I find that astonishing, so many countries that are the centre of religion, greed, feuding etc. Then little old Iceland, troubling nobody, until their volcanoes erupted and covered so many of us with their ash and didn't the financial crash start there? I just thought that little "I" was interesting.

If this has resonated with you and you do begin to make a start in praying for the world Jesus loves, then I know God will draw very close to you and your prayer life will be greatly enriched.

Okay then, time to get off that postage stamp and pray for the world Jesus gave his life for.

* * *

4. BARS AND STARS

During this time of self-isolation and social exclusion my mind turned to a story I heard years ago about bars and stars, which I have not been able to verify, but the lesson remains true for us today in our lockdown or lockup situations.

The story I was told was that Winston Churchill, then a young war correspondent, was captured and imprisoned in South Africa during the Boer War. There were two prisoners in the cell, Winston and one other man. The other man became depressed because all he could see were the bars of the prison cell. On the other hand, Winston became increasingly restless and agitated as he paced around the cell. He looked out and instead of seeing bars, he saw the stars which represented his destiny and the call which he knew was on his life. Below is an extract from *The Daring Escape That Forged Winston Churchill* by Christopher Klein.

Winston Churchill, the young war correspondent was among those captured by the Boers and transported to a prisoner-of-war camp in the enemy capital of Pretoria.

"There is no ambition I cherish so keenly as to gain a reputation for personal courage," Churchill had confided to his younger brother, Jack, two years earlier. As tales of his bravery reached London, that reputation was finally his, but it came at the price of his freedom. Although the Boers allowed prisoners-of-war to purchase newspapers, cigarettes and beer, the future prime minister despised his imprisonment "more than I have ever hated any other period in my whole life." What frustrated Churchill even more than the loss of control was the possibility that he was missing out on further opportunities for glory. "I had only cut myself out of the whole of this exciting war with all its boundless possibilities of adventure and advancement," he lamented.

On the night of December 12, 1899, while the guards weren't watching, Churchill scaled the prison fence and made a break for freedom. The fugitive may have had no map, no ability to speak the local language and just "four slabs of melting chocolate and a crumbling biscuit" in his pocket, but he still possessed a seemingly superhuman level of self-belief that he could safely navigate the 300-miles journey through enemy territory. As the Boers launched a massive manhunt—posters offered a reward for his capture, "dead or alive"—Britain became captivated by Churchill's saga.

A thrilling story, I think you will agree, but what grips me is the strong inner belief that Churchill had concerning his future destiny of being Prime Minister to Great Britain and of achieving greatness.

Winston Churchill had a warrior spirit and a fierce determination to succeed in whatever he set his hand to do. That inner strength was born out of what some of us might call a prophetic word even though it was from a questionable source. The fact is that the words spoken into him as a young man, concerning his future greatness, drove him on and fired him up during times of adversity. Single-minded in every way, Churchill would not take "No" for an answer.

Now for you and me today, shut up, locked away for who knows how many weeks, what do you see? The bars of confinement and restriction to your freedom, or the stars in the night sky?

There is a life and a destiny that awaits each one of us and this is but a training ground for that. Allow this precious time of quiet to shape and mold you into the person you are going to be in the immediate and long-term future. God says, if you put your life in His hands, there are no restrictions, no limits and nothing which is impossible for you. Take time now to listen to the still small voice of God in your heart, let him speak those words of love and healing deep into you, read some great literature to inspire you and get ready to go for gold when the shackles come off.

* * *

5. BIG DOORS SWING ON SMALL HINGES (Part 1)

I recall being invited to speak at a celebration service in Rochdale. This was a big meeting in the town because the invite went out to all of the local churches, whatever their label. I actually love those kind of events where Christians come together from their various traditions, as one. I know that God loves it too.

Anyway, we were well into the service coming close to when I was due to speak. Suddenly I began to feel uneasy about the message I had prepared and as sharp as an arrow (not that I know personally what that feels like!) this phrase came to me, "Big doors swing on small hinges". Within myself I said, "What does that mean?" and straightaway I knew that was what I had to speak on. I had nothing else, but I sensed God was saying, "You open your mouth and I will fill it".

Soon my turn came to speak, and after the usual pleasantries, I simply began by announcing, "The title of tonight's message is Big Doors Swing on Small Hinges". I honestly cannot remember much of what I said but it was to the effect that Jesus is the door and, if we come to him and enter in through Him, then that door would expose us to the miraculous and God would do things for us beyond our wildest dreams.

At the end of the meeting I invited people who wanted to come forward for a prayer of blessing, or to give their lives to Jesus for the very first time, to do so.

Quite a few people came forward and there was a small team helping me to pray for people.

What stood out for me though was a husband and wife, who told me they had been trying to have children for a long time, but they had been told it was unlikely they would ever conceive. They told me, however, that the message had been spot on for them and they believed a big door had swung open that night and they were now in faith that they would have children.

A year or so later I visited another church in Rochdale and I was told the great news that the couple in question had in fact now been blessed with a child of their own. Years later I heard that the same couple gave a testimony at a Bible Camp in Lincoln explaining their miracle and I think, by that time, they had four children!

I am so glad, on that evening, I was obedient to what I believe was the prompting of the Holy Spirit. It was exciting to receive a message like that, which I had not prepared but which was so full of life.

Looking back over my life, I can now recognize many occasions when what at the time seemed like a small decision, opened up a big door for me.

The most spectacular came in the workplace. One day a young lady walked past my desk and then, almost as an afterthought, came back to me and said, "John, I put together the monthly office magazine. We are short of articles this time around, so would you consider writing something for us?"

"What would you like me to write about?" I asked.

She thought for a moment and said, "How about writing about the challenges you face as a person with a disability in the workplace and how you deal with the constant changes in such a positive manner".

I thought for a moment and said, "Okay, I will give it a go and email something to you".

Well, I am so glad I responded like that rather than saying I have never done anything like that before.

This was a small hinge that was about to open a big door for me. I wrote the article and it was so well received, especially by one of our Area Directors. He was so amazed by it, he took me under his wing, invested in my personal development and ultimately that led to me making Diversity and Inspirational talks right across the country to Civil Servants of all grades. This led to me being awarded an MBE in the 2014 Queen's Birthday Honours List.

In conclusion, therefore, let me encourage you to keep your eyes open for opportunities to do new things and to step out of your comfort zone. You just never know, by saying yes to that seemingly little invitation, a big door may be opening in your life.

* * *

6. BIG DOORS SWING ON SMALL HINGES (Part 2)

In my previous article I was explaining how sometimes seemingly insignificant decisions we take can lead to massive doors of opportunity opening up for us.

Another such time in my life was after Sylvia had finished reading to me a book called, *The New Johnny Cash*. The book was a biography detailing how Johnny had been able to turn his life around, following his marriage to June Carter. The power of June's love for Johnny gave him the strength to leave alcohol, and a dependency on prescription drugs behind, and return to his Christian roots.

I found the book to be so inspiring I wanted everyone to read it. I came up with the idea of contacting the presenter of the country music show on the local BBC radio station. Ken Dudeney was the host of *Keep it Country* broadcast weekly on what was then Radio Birmingham. I wrote a letter, explaining how much I loved the book and could it be reviewed on his show. Well imagine my surprise when a few days later, Ken rang me up and said that as I had clearly loved the book so much, why didn't I go in and review it myself on the show?

This was exciting and the following Wednesday I took myself off into Birmingham and then out to the old Pebble Mill studios. I found my way to the reception where Ken was actually waiting for me. He was quite taken aback to see that I had a white stick, and he apologized to me saying that he had not realised I was visually impaired.

Once the shock was over, we made our way to the studio with me holding on to his arm. This was great; I had always wanted to be involved in radio in some way. In no time at all I was sat in the studio with a headset on. Ken said he would do the book review in an interview style.

Well, I enjoyed hearing some of my favourite country records and, when the time came for the interview, I thought it went really well and more-to-the-point so did Ken. After the programme, we went for a coffee in the BBC canteen and that is where things became interesting. I talked about my love of Country and Gospel music and of some of the albums I had in my collection. Ken then came up with a great idea.

He said, "Shortly we will be coming up to Easter, so why don't we do a special show? You could bring in eight of your favourite Country Gospel album tracks and explain to the listeners what they mean to you".

My heart thumped with excitement at the prospect. This for me was a dream come true. Playing music that I loved and with a Gospel message too. I could hardly wait.

The time came for the show and, excited as I was, it all went fabulously well and we had a great response from listeners. Ken was so impressed he offered me a regular spot on his show to feature Country Gospel music.

I did that for a few years and then the station, which became BBC WM, underwent a major change of schedules. All of the specialist music programmes were discarded in favour of a more generic approach. I was told they did not want to lose me, so I was being invited to review new Christian music on a new Sunday morning show called *A Word in Advance* with Rev Michael Blood. All in all, I did that for about 12 years. Michael and I had a great rapport in the studio and people often said that as much as they loved the music, they liked our banter even more.

Over the years I have also done some broadcasts for BBC Radio 4, Radio Devon and Radio Cornwall as well as BRMB, the former commercial station in Birmingham.

To think that none of this may ever have happened had Sylvia not read that book to me and my response been, "I want to share this with more people".

As I said in my previous article, these seemingly small decisions in life could well open a big door of opportunity for you. I was once at a seminar with a senior business leader and, when he was asked what was the first thing he looked for in a potential leader, his answer was enthusiasm. If you feel enthusiastic about something, don't lock it up, but let it overflow as that may be the little hinge that will open a big door for you.

* * *

7. BITE IT AND BELIEVE IT

Today, let us think about chocolate. I know Easter is now well past and the chocolate eggs in your family are probably long gone, but it's still a nice subject for most of us in the midst of troubled times. I wonder what your personal favourite chocolate treat would be? I cannot claim to be a chocolate addict, but I do have the occasional fads on a Mars Bar, Crunchie, Galaxy and a few others besides. If you could pin me down to name a favourite, however, I guess I would say Whisper. I like the fact that it's light and fluffy with a pleasing texture and taste.

Whisper is quite unusual of course because, although it was brought out in the 1980s, it was withdrawn from manufacture later due to a drop in sales. It was, thankfully, relaunched after an Internet campaign to bring it back.

When it was first launched though, can you recall what it's advertising slogan was? Well it was none other than "Bite It and Believe It".

From the beginning, I loved that strapline. Straightaway it reminded me of a short passage in the Old Testament of The Bible.

Ezekiel 3 [New International Version]

And he said to me, "Son of man, eat what is before you, eat this scroll; then go and speak to the people of Israel." So I opened my mouth, and he gave me the scroll to eat.

Then he said to me, "Son of man, eat this scroll I am giving you and fill your stomach with it." So I ate it, and it tasted as sweet as honey in my mouth.

The scroll, of course, contained the Holy Scriptures and it would not have been the normal thing to eat it! Ezekiel, however, the obedient servant of God, took the scroll and ate it. Incredibly as he did so, it became as sweet as honey in his mouth. He filled his stomach with it.

Now this is an example to us to take the Word of God and, whilst not physically eating it, we are encouraged to meditate on God's Word day and night. As I understand it, that means to read it, recite it, memorize it, think on it, ponder it and saver it. Literally, like cattle chewing the cud. Imagine Ezekiel chewing that scroll and then swallowing it until it became as sweet as honey in his mouth.

The Word of God can become to you the sweetest thing in life providing you take the time to draw out its nutrients. I used to be under the misguided impression that I read God's Word for His benefit. It was quite a revelation to discover God's Word is there for my instruction, guidance, comfort, faith and so many other things. The benefits to knowing God's Word are enumerable, but the onus is on you and me to "Bite it and Believe it". Then God will send us out, as he did with Ezekiel to let the whole world know.

* * *

8. BLACK IS BLACK

Regular readers to my posts will know that music often features and today is no exception. Apologies to my younger readers that a lot of my songs go back somewhat, reflecting my age. Keep your eyes open though because I do also like some more modern music so you just never know, your favourite song may yet get a mention.

Black is Black was a hit song in the 1960s, recorded by a Spanish band called Los Lobos. My dear late wife told me that she found the lead singer to be, in her words, "Rather attractive".

The song, though fairly upbeat in style lyrically is somewhat of a lament as the man is singing about a lost love and, as a result, everything to him seemed black.

I guess we all go through times like that and maybe that has been you during this time of lockdown.

Generally speaking, I have been doing pretty well, with a good routine in place every day. This week, however, has been one of the blackest weeks of my life. A really tough time for reasons it would not be right to go into here. The spirit can be lifted as we watch, listen or read about heroic acts in the face of the pandemic – who will ever forget 99-year-old Captain Tom Moore and his heroic efforts, walking with a frame around his garden to raise money for the NHS. Tom's initial target was £1,000, but as most of you will know the figure has astonishingly gone to over £30 million.

As good and uplifting as all that is, however, it does nothing to change the difficult circumstances in which I find myself. Here again you may be able to identify if you are in a sad, desperate situation that you do not have the power to change.

I am a Christian, though, and I find great encouragement from the Bible and having God's Word living in my heart. Believe me, there are hundreds of encouraging Scriptures, but I have chosen just one for now.

In the Old Testament of the Bible one of the minor prophets (so called not because he was of less importance than the others, but more because he had fewer prophesies than people like Jeremiah and Isaiah) was in a dire situation. Talk about Black is Black. Habakkuk is his name and just read what he had to contend with:

Habakkuk 3:17-18 New International Version

Though the fig tree does not bud
  and there are no grapes on the vines,
though the olive crop fails
  and the fields produce no food,
though there are no sheep in the pen
  and no cattle in the stalls,
yet I will rejoice in the LORD,
  I will be joyful in God my Saviour.

When everything in your world seems to be spiralling out of control, you are locked in and cannot do anything about it, Habakkuk (don't you just love that name!) gives us the answer. Everything in Habakkuk's life was going wrong, nothing was working, but he chose to say, "Yet I will rejoice in the Lord always, I will be joyful in God my Saviour."

In my life nothing outwardly has changed, the issues I faced at the beginning of the week are still staring me in the face but, like the wonderfully named Habakkuk, I have chosen to sing praises to my Lord Jesus Christ and trust him for a good outcome. May I encourage you to do the same if your situation seems blacker than black.

* * *

9. CAN I BE "SELFISH" AND EXPECT GOD TO BLESS ME?

Parental logic has often been questioned by puzzled children. The classic one, of course, is when children are wide awake at night and they are made to go to bed; then when they are fast asleep in the morning, they are forced to wake up to go to school. Then there were times I would ask my Mum for something, possibly for more dinner, or a biscuit, but she would say, "No, it's rude to ask, so because of that you cannot have one".

I was known to respond by saying, "Well, if I don't ask how do you know what I want?" and that would probably result in a slap for being so cheeky as to answer back.

Of course, we live in very different days now and children, as I understand it, are encouraged to be more vocal and express what they are feeling. Obviously there are risks with that, but overall, I think it's a good thing and certainly the Bible indicates that our Heavenly Father is like that.

Some years ago, I decided to attempt the mammoth task of reading the Bible from Genesis to Revelation in braille. Quite a task as braille-reading was never my strong point. Anyway, I ploughed on with the task, managing to work my way painstakingly through the begetting chapters and all of those long names. I made my way to 1 Chronicles, struggled up to chapter four and gave up; the sequence of more and more names was just too much for me.

Later, a friend asked me how I was doing with reading the Bible from Genesis and I had to admit defeat, declaring that I had given up at 1 Chronicles 4 because I was weary of struggling to read the list of names. "That's a pity", my friend said, "if you had persevered you would have come to a gem".

I enquired what this gem was, and he pointed me to 1 Chronicles 4:10, the prayer of Jabez. He told me that the name Jabez meant "the sorrow-maker" because his mother bore him in pain and sadness. When Jabez grew up, however, there was a deep yearning in his heart to know the God of his ancestors and so he cried out from his innermost being to the God of Israel saying, "Oh Lord please bless me and enlarge my borders, keep your hand upon me to guide me and keep me from sin, so that it may not harm me". The next verse goes on to say, "God was pleased to grant him that which he requested". 1 Chronicles then carries on with the list of names and generations, but that one golden nugget is tucked away there for anyone who is serious about reading God's Word to find it.

God was clearly blessed enough to include that prayer in the Holy Scriptures and even though it was a very selfish prayer, God answered it with pleasure.

Six times in one short prayer, Jabez uses the words "me" or "my", but God did not seem to mind one jot. We know that God looks on the heart and here was a man who was aching for God's presence. He cried out from the very pit of his stomach for God to bless him and increase his sphere of influence. Jabez was clearly not sitting on his laurels, he desperately wanted to develop his potential whilst at the same time knowing God's guidance and protection from the temptations of sin.

Jesus said, "Ask and you will receive, seek and you will find, knock and the door will be opened to you". It's all about persistence and making yourself a nuisance as you come before the Lord. In Luke 11 we read about the person who comes knocking on the door at midnight, demanding bread. "What a pest," we think, but God seems to encourage this attitude when it comes to prayer. I think God wants to see how determined we are. James says in his letter that we have not, because we ask not, and then he goes on to talk about the effective, fervent prayer of a righteous man achieves much. I am told that the word "fervent" literally means "white hot" and that's pretty warm!

If, like me therefore, you have been brought up to be more passive and that it's rude to ask, think again. It's time to get passionate and white hot and, like Jabez, cry out to God from the pit of your stomach for God to bless you and anoint you afresh with his Spirit so you may fully realise your potential as a child of God. Don't look around to see where others are at and what they are doing. It's time to be selfish and receive the blessing God has for you.

Be like Jacob and don't let go until God blesses you.

* * *

10. CATERPILLARS AND BUTTERFLIES

A fear of death is not normally something you associate with young children, but it was certainly true of me. I am not really sure how it came about, but there was a close family friend who killed herself by putting her head in the gas oven. Apparently in 1950s Britain, this was quite a common form of suicide. I am sure that contributed in some way to my dread of even thinking about the subject of death. I did what a lot of people do and tried to ignore it.

Growing up in Birmingham, much of my time was taken up with playing football in the street - morning, noon and night. I loved it. As a side-line, in Spring and Summer I enjoyed collecting caterpillars. At one point I think I had four jam jars with a caterpillar in each one. I took pride in caring for them, regularly changing the grass and leaves inside the jar. Each day I would let the caterpillars out for a run around. I had been told that eventually the caterpillar would climb to the top of the jar and stick itself to the lid, in which I had pierced small holes to help them breathe. It was just amazing to me to watch. Over a few days, the caterpillar would die and change into a chrysalis and then a small gap would appear in the shell. This was the sign for me to turn the lid upside down in readiness for the butterfly to emerge. What an incredible sight it was to watch as that fragile butterfly, so beautifully coloured, emerged from that chrysalis and fly gracefully into the sky. I really did find it all quite emotional.

Even at that tender age I can remember having a fleeting thought, "I wonder if that is what happens to us when we die?" but I would quickly brush away the thought, because I did not want to go down that death road. Below is a paragraph I have found on a website, which puts it far better than I can.

"Biologically speaking, the change of a caterpillar into a butterfly is spoken of as a "metamorphosis." The ugly, repulsive caterpillar is confined to a tomb which it spins for itself. While in the cocoon there is an apparently dead and formless substance. But after the warm sun of spring has beaten its golden rays upon that cocoon, there comes forth a beautiful butterfly. Though the butterfly is different in appearance from the caterpillar, we recognize the beautiful winged insect as being the same as the caterpillar. It is the same living creature, yet different. So also is the resurrection of the body."

In the traditional Church calendar, the week before Easter is known as Holy Week, which remembers the journey of Jesus into Jerusalem to endure a mock trial and then be crucified on what we call Good Friday. Then, just as Jesus said would be the case, He was raised from the dead on Sunday morning.

In creation we see trees, flowers and plants dying off in the Autumn and Winter, but come Spring they begin to burst into life so that by the Summer they are in full bloom once again, so the cycle of life-death and life continue.

That being the case, is it unreasonable to assume that we as human-beings, just like the humble caterpillar-butterfly scenario, will follow the same course?

God has said that we are the highest of all his creation and for those who love and put their trust in Jesus, He has promised that we will have everlasting life. Jesus himself said, when He stood at the tomb of his friend Lazarus, "I am the resurrection and the life; he though he were dead, yet shall he live".

I am sure you will agree that the butterfly is many times more attractive than the caterpillar. Jesus has promised that when we, who believe and trust in him, are raised from the dead we will have glorious new bodies. " ... by the power that enables Him to bring everything under His control, will transform our lowly bodies so that they will be like His glorious body." (Philippians 3:21)

For me, the fear of death left me the moment I prayed and invited Jesus to come and live in my heart as my Lord and Saviour. Over 50 years have come and gone since then and with the hymn-writer I can say, "You ask me how I know He lives – He lives within my heart".

From now on, when you see a butterfly, remind yourself that the beautiful creature you see was born out of death and then think on those things for a while. This may well lead to you considering the Easter message of Jesus' death and resurrection and what that could mean for you. You could for instance, invite Jesus to exchange your old life for a beautiful new one, just like the butterfly. "If anyone becomes a Christian, they are a new creation, the old things have passed away and the new has come." (2 Corinthians 5:17)

* * *

11. DONKEY RIDE, ANYONE?

We all have childhood memories. Hopefully, many more good ones than bad.

One of the highlights for me, my brother and two sisters was our annual holiday to Blackpool. As a family together with Mum and Dad we had some fabulous times there. One of the standout memories from those wonderful holidays were the obligatory donkey rides on the beach. They were so much fun; even selecting the donkey each one of us wanted to ride on.

In the traditional Christian Church, Holy Week is celebrated in the lead up to Easter culminating in the death and resurrection of Jesus from the dead. At the beginning of that week, Jesus took a donkey ride into Jerusalem.

You can read the story in Matthew 21 of the Bible and I suggest you read it in a modern version, such as The Message Bible.

In the account you will note that the donkey and colt in question were tied up. It might be that is a picture of you, bound up in fear, anxiety, sickness, addiction, grief etc. Jesus instructed his two friends to loose the animals and set them free. That is exactly what Jesus wants to do for you and me all the time. He is constantly in the business of setting us free to be what we were created to be.

Then Jesus went for his donkey ride into the City. Incredibly, that humble donkey carried the Son of God and brought His presence into Jerusalem.

I truly believe that God is looking for people who are bound up, broken and hurting so that He can heal and release them to be what they were destined to be. Having set us free, He then says to us, "Now will you carry my presence into your family, street, village, town or city?"

One of the things Jesus said about himself was, "I am the light of the world". When you invite Jesus to come into your life to liberate you, he puts his Divine light on the inside of you. You and I then have the privilege of letting that brilliant light shine in all the world.

"Let your light so shine before people that they may see your good works and glorify your Father in Heaven." (Matthew 5:16)

Now, where are those old holiday photographs?

* * *

12. EXCITE GOD!

Prayer is so vital to our Christian life and at this time of severe lockdown, social distancing and isolation, the business of prayer has come more sharply into focus.

Have you noticed how some days prayer is so easy, yet other days it really is tough and you have to work hard at it before you feel you are getting through to a listening, compassionate God? Again, this should not be surprising because, as we are aware, we do have an enemy who does not want us to be in direct communication with our Heavenly Father.

Many years ago, I was made aware of a poster outside a church, which read, "Life is Fragile - Handle with Prayer". Well for many, life has never felt so fragile as it does today, so let me share some things with you about prayer that may encourage you.

About four years ago, one January morning, I was on my knees pouring my heart out to God and basically saying, "I am bored with my prayer life".

Imagine my astonishment, when immediately into my spirit came this reply, "So am I".

With this, Father God had my attention and I sensed him reminding me of what it is like when I am at a football match. People are sitting down watching the game, but when anything really exciting starts to happen then everyone gets up off their seats. It was as though God was saying to me, "Pray prayers that will excite me and get me off my seat". Well, what a challenge that is!

"Now to Him (God) who is ready, willing and able to do immeasurably more than we can ask, think or even imagine, according to the mighty resurrection power that is within us, be glory in the Church." (Ephesians 3:20) – slightly amplified John Flanner version, but I am assured this is what the verse is actually saying.

Can I ask you to meditate on that verse and allow its power and implication to sink deep into your heart? How much are you asking God for, how much are you thinking on it and how much are you imagining what God can do in your life and the lives of others?

I know, beyond a shadow of doubt, that there is so much more to prayer than we have yet discovered. Jesus' disciples were very religious. They had been brought up to pray as devout Jews, yet when they heard Jesus praying their response was, "Lord, teach us to pray". Maybe we should be in that place of humility and asking Jesus to help us to go deeper in prayer.

In the late 1980s I used to attend an early morning prayer meeting at a Bible College. There were usually about 20 people present and the purpose of the meeting was to pray for the nations of the world. In one month, we planned to cover the whole world with our prayers. We had a prayer plan whereby we read up about eight different nations each day and brought them before the Lord along with their national leaders. It was exciting and exhilarating as we marched up and down, praying in English and in tongues as the Holy Spirit led us. During those times God even gave me a couple of songs, which was incredible to me. We certainly prayed with a lot of fervour helped, in no small measure, by the fact that in our number were quite a few men and women from Ghana and Nigeria and they really did know how to pray with passion. I loved those meetings and felt God stretched me to a new level.

Praying for the nations certainly made me more aware of world events and the joy that I felt in 1989 when apartheid was broken in South Africa, the Berlin Wall came down in Germany, Communism crumbled in the USSR and in Czechoslovakia. While not wishing to take all the credit of course, I had a sense that our small prayer group so full of passion, did play a part. I think we excited God and 'got him off his seat' on that occasion.

A short while later, one of those African students came to me and said he was going to pray through the night because he needed a financial breakthrough. The student was named Alex and he asked me if I would join him. I felt honoured and a little nervous to be honest. Well the night in question came and I left home at about 10pm. I joined Alex and we began to pray sitting down. Before too long Alex was up, marching the floor praying in tongues. Not wishing to be left out, I joined him, and we prayed for a long time. At first it was tough but it became easier and there was a sense of riding on the wind, as it were. Sometimes we prayed in English, sometimes in tongues and sometimes we sang praises to God. It was incredible, and the time just flew by. Then at about 2.30am Alex tapped me on the shoulder and said, "That's it, brother, we have the breakthrough".

Well, I have to say that Alex must have been more in tune with the Holy Spirit than me, because I did not sense anything any different.

When I arrived home and crawled into bed, a very sleepy Sylvia said, "You're back early, I thought you were praying all night".

"We were," I said, "but we got the breakthrough", and we drifted off to sleep.

I had been praying about a need we had, because our car had developed a major mechanical problem. What a pleasant surprise, then, when just a couple of days later we received an anonymous gift of £1,000. God had answered the prayers spectacularly. Alex was right, we did get the breakthrough, well at least we did for us.

Sylvia and I agreed to tithe the money and to give it to Alex towards his needs. When I gave it to him, Alex gave me a massive bear hug and bounced me up and down, shouting "Hallelujah!" at the top of his voice, exclaiming, "This is the exact amount I was praying for".

So what prayers are you going to pray that will get God 'off his seat' with excitement. Remember He is the God of whom it is said, nothing is impossible. One prayer I have been praying, is this. In my family there are four of us who are registered blind. I have asked God to stretch out his hand, rest a finger on each one of us and heal us all at the same time, wherever we are in the country. Too hard for God? No way.

Bring it on Lord!

* * *

13. FOOTBALL AND HEAVEN

One of the most famous quotes attributed to the legendary former Liverpool manager, Bill Shankly is, *"Some people think football is a matter of life and death. I don't like that attitude. I can assure them it is much more serious than that".*

I am sure that comment was a bit tongue in cheek, but just in case there are any of the gravelly-voiced Glaswegian's disciples reading this, I have to say that the comment is totally untrue. Football, as with many other sports, does have the ability to create a massive emotional swing, leaving one either on a mountain top of shear ecstasy or deep in the valley of despair. It is not uncommon to experience both extremes of emotion within a few moments of each other. For all that, however, football is not a matter of life and death. It is most definitely a sport, a means of recreation and social intercourse. It must be added that, for some who are in the game professionally, a series of poor results can cost them their job. Even that, though serious, is nowhere near as important as life and death.

It is so easy for sport to become an all-consuming passion and I know that only too well. It has to be said though that the questions of life and death, such as "Why are we here?", "What happens when we die?" and "Is there a Heaven and a Hell?" remain of paramount importance to every person on the planet. These days there is a lot of talk about combatting the threat of terrorism but, to be perfectly honest, the one terrorist every single one of us will have to face one day is death itself.

The amusing story is told of one football nut who could not stand the thought of dying and going to Heaven if there was no football. To deal with this predicament, he did something I would actively discourage in that he went to a fortune teller. Going behind the curtain he said to the lady, "I love football and I am desperate to know if there is football in Heaven".

She admitted that she had never received such a strange request before, so excused herself while she went to consult her crystal ball. On her return she said, "Well I have good news and bad news, so which would you like to hear first?"

"The good news", the man said.

"The good news is there is most definitely football in Heaven".

"That's great," the man said, "so what is the bad news?"

The fortune teller responded, "You are playing in Match of the Day on Saturday night!"

What a shock for the enthusiast of the beautiful game! Now let me state this. I have no idea whether they play football in Heaven or not, but I am convinced there is a Heaven to gain and a Hell to shun, as someone once put it.

I first learned about Heaven in Sunday School – some of you will remember that now seemingly outdated tradition. My belief in Heaven was further deepened in school assemblies, because every day we said, "The Lord's Prayer". In the midst of those 69 amazing words we said "Our Father in Heaven…. Your Kingdom come on Earth as it is in Heaven. Thus, my confidence that there was a Heaven was developed in my formative years. Later I discovered that Jesus spoke about the Kingdom of Heaven too.

My question, therefore, is how do I get to go to this incredible place where the Bible tells us there is no pain, no tears, no war and incidentally no marriage. Of course, I, along with you will have to die, but after that, does everyone get to go to Heaven?

That's a brilliant question, which sadly myriads of people fail to ask. For many years I assumed that if there was a Heaven and if God is a God of love then we will all make it. I now say quite categorically that is not true, at least according to Jesus and the Bible.

One of the most famous verses in the entire Bible, John chapter 3 verse 16 says "For God the Father so loved this world that whoever believes and trusts in Jesus Christ as their Lord and Saviour, will not die but will have everlasting life in heaven". That is my slightly expanded version of the verse just to make it obvious to all.

Let's put it like this: you don't get to enjoy Heaven, and all its benefits, by accident or happenstance. Rather, Heaven is a choice you make. Suppose for instance you want to attend the next FA Cup Final. In order to be there you will need a ticket. No ticket no entry. Heaven is like that too.

Unlike the FA Cup Final though and other all-ticket events, there is no limit on the number of people who can go to Heaven. In fact, the Bible says that God is not willing for anyone to miss out. He loves the world and people he created so much that he wants everyone to be there. So desperate is He for everyone to be there, including you, that Jesus Christ, God's Son came to die a horrible death on a cross so that we could all be there. The point is though that you do need a ticket, or at least an equivalent. In order to get into Heaven, you need a name and that name is Jesus Christ. Again, quoting the Bible which says, there is no other name given among mankind, by which mankind can be saved. The name is Jesus. It is like me trying to gain access to your computer. I cannot do it without a password. We cannot gain access to God's Heaven without that name. How good of God. He has not kept his password secret, but made it known to the whole world – it is Jesus Christ and he has commanded his followers to trumpet blast that name around the world so that the entire world has the opportunity of being saved and going to Heaven to enjoy eternal life.

Many people of course would argue that there are many ways to Heaven, but that is not what Jesus said. Again, in the Bible in the Gospel of John chapter 14 Jesus was talking to some of his followers about his impending death. He knew that he was going to die on a tree for the sins of the world but, not surprisingly, his friends did not grasp it and they were worried. Jesus then said "Do not let your heart be troubled. You believe in God, that's good, now believe in me also. In my Father's house are many villas. I will go and prepare a villa for you so that where I am you may be also." The word villa of course is often translated mansion or large room, but as this is an article about my passion, I think villa will suffice!

Jesus went on to say the immortal words, "I am the way, the truth and the life, no one can come to the Father in Heaven except through me."

There you have it then. It cannot be put any clearer. That one statement, more than any other, got Jesus crucified. The Jews hated that, calling it blasphemy, because they were waiting for their Messiah. They were too blind to see that he was there in the midst of them. They actually killed the very one who came to save them. Thankfully, Jesus rose again from the dead, unlike any other religious leader I have ever heard of, and He lives today to bring eternal life to anyone who will put their trust in him. The Bible uses another word familiar to football supporters saying that Jesus became our substitute. I now realise that when Jesus died on that cross, he did so to become my substitute. Again, I quote some well-known verses from the Bible.

"All have sinned and fallen short of God's perfect standard and the wages of sin is death, but the free gift of God is eternal life".

"He who has the Son of God has life, but he who does not have the Son does not have life."

So, you see the great Bill Shankly did not have it right after all. Life and death are important. How we live in the here and now is important and how we die is vital also. If we die with Christ, then we are guaranteed everlasting life.

So, seeing beyond the beautiful game, what's the score with you? Next time you sing the Cup Final Hymn, *Abide With Me*, when it comes to the line, "In life and death, Oh Lord, Abide with me," maybe you could sing it from the depth of your heart and mean it.

* * *

14. GETTING TO KNOW YOU

As I awoke this morning there was a melody deep within me. I opened my mouth and began to hum it. To my surprise I recognized it was *Getting to Know You*, one of the show-stoppings songs from the smash hit musical *The King and I*.

I reflected on the movie that I first saw way back in the early 1960s which starred Yul Brynner and Deborah Kerr. I found myself being thankful to God for the first 19 years of my life when I could see perfectly, and my mind recalled the stunning visual images from that movie.
My memory of watching the film helped me recall the joy and wonder of those hundred or more Siamese children as they learned

so much from their teacher Miss Anna. Anna was having to learn and adapt to her new culture, while the children were discovering things outside of themselves that previously they never knew existed. I love it in the movie too when Anna is teaching the King to dance. Those joyous visual images fill my head even now over 50 years on from when I first saw them as Anna and the King learn to dance energetically together.

At this time of enforced isolation Jesus, the King of all Kings and the Lord of all Lords, is wanting to become more closely acquainted with us. Everything else has been stripped away so that we can get to know Him afresh, in a deeper way, or for the very first time.

My daughter Beverley said to me that she has really enjoyed this last week off work because it has enabled her to spend time with her husband, Phil. They both have time-consuming and demanding jobs, which means that their time together is often at a premium.

The Bible declares "God is Love". That means he is a lover, the greatest of all, by the way. He loves in a way so as not to abuse those He created. So, with those pictures from the King and I uppermost in our minds, let me encourage you to get to know the King and learn to dance to the beat of his heart.

By the way, it's well over 50 years now that I have been physically blind, but it has been said to me at the beginning of this year by a respected friend from Hillsong in Australia that I am going to receive my eyesight. I have said I will see him in Australia when I go across there to give my testimony and, I tell you what, I may just take another look at the King and I because I am sure I will be dancing too.

Finally, along the theme I have been talking about, let me recommend that you listen to a song on YouTube called *Teach Me to Dance* by Graham Kendrick. It explains so well what I am talking about in this article. Now Dance on … but that's another tune for another time!

* * *

15. GOD KNOWS WHAT HE'S DOING

After going blind at the age of 19, I found myself at a rehabilitation centre in Torquay for 12 weeks in the glorious summer of 1967. It was my first time away from home and it was very scary to begin with. The point of the course was to develop new skills, such as reading braille, learning to type, basics in woodwork and metalwork etc. The purpose of all of this was to assess what kind of work, if any, I would be suitable for.

Computer programming was the big new thing and I fancied that because I loved working with numbers. During the last week of the course, I was given an appointment to go and sit before a three-person committee and receive the verdict. Quite honestly, I was expecting to hear, "Sorry John, we do not feel you have the necessary skills for employment, so we will assign you to a social worker for follow up". That was the fate which awaited most of the 72 newly blind people on the course. My ears pricked up, however, when the meeting began with "John, we have good news for you…."

My dreams were quickly shattered, however, when the chairman of the panel continued, "We have assessed your overall skills and have decided to send you to London to train as an audio typist".

I had a terrifying fear of girls though and, as the only typists I knew were female, this was not good news in my book.

I spent the next few months worrying about my impending nine-month stay in London and meeting those terrifying women.

I need not have worried though, although my typing teacher Mrs Craig, was very strict. Without me realizing it, God already had his hand on my life in a wonderful way and it was that same Mrs Craig, who first talked with me about Jesus and the need to be, in Jesus' words, "Born again".

1968 was a great year for me. I began at Pembridge Place Commercial College for the blind on 1st January; met my three roommates who would become great friends (all male I hasten to add); had my 21st birthday in July; and on 28 December, met the beautiful young lady who would become my wife. I also had a wonderful time in London, enjoying the restaurants, bars and going out to some of the soul music clubs with my new friends.

Something else happened that year too, which totally transformed me as a person, and how I looked on myself. As I said earlier, Mrs Craig, (Molly if you should want to know her Christian name) had talked with me about Jesus and what it really meant to be a Christian, as opposed to just being born in England and being christened as a baby, which is what I thought a Christian was. I was introduced to two of Mrs Craig's friends, Tony and Margaret, both themselves blind. I was invited by them to attend a service at Westminster Chapel and that is where it happened for me. The singing was amazing and so inspirational and so too was the preacher. The message was so clear as he explained the good news about Jesus from the beautiful book of Ruth in the Bible. Somehow everything slotted into place and as I later realised, it was as though all of the lemons lined up on the one-armed bandit, and I got the jackpot! I saw it, it all became clear to me, Jesus loved me, and my response was simply to say "yes" to him and invite him to fill me with His love.

An old friend of mine, Bob Gilman, who wrote the well-known Christian song *Bind us Together*, has written and recorded many other songs. One of them, that I love, goes:

"Jesus you're terrific, I really think you are
You took me from the dustbin, now you treat me like a star
Jesus you're terrific, that's what I call good news
Though you're the King of everything, to love me still you choose."

Hardly the most eloquent poetry, but in it's stark and simple truth it is so powerfully dynamic. I love it so much because that is exactly what Jesus did for me and will do for anyone. I did feel as though he had taken me from the dustbin, where I thought I was rubbish, useless, ugly, and untalented, but now God had lavished his love upon me. Jesus, the King of the universe, had chosen to love me and it was truly an amazing revelation, one I have never lost.

Sometimes in life I do find it hard to pray but, as far as I can recall, I have hardly found it hard to praise him because Jesus really is terrific.

As for the typing bit, I passed my exams with flying colours, overcame my fear of girls and have gone on to write much including publishing three books before this one.

I guess that God knew what he was doing after all!

* * *

16. GUIDE DOG TO GUIDE GOD

From time to time in life we are called upon to have to make some very tough decisions and in January 2019, one of those times came my way.

With my wife Sylvia suffering from dementia and being totally bedbound, after discussing with my family, I decided to apply for a guide dog. I have never owned a dog before, so this was a massive step, but we felt the dog would not only help me regain some independence but would also be a great companion for Sylvia.

After a wait of more than a year I was invited to the Guide Dog Centre in Leamington Spa and, shortly afterwards, a suitable match was found. I was going to take ownership of Eaton, a beautiful 18-month-old black Labrador/Golden Retriever. Immediately Eaton won the hearts of all of my family members and friends.

We began our training and all went well although, I have to say that for me, it was one of the most difficult learning experiences I have ever undertaken. After 50 years being blind and getting around using a white stick, it was so difficult to relax and trust Eaton to lead me. The idea was to hold the handle on the harness very lightly and be led by the messages that were coming to me via that handle. To begin with I was so much in control that I was leading the dog and then my hand was so tightly gripped around the handle that my trainer could see the tension all over me.

Eventually though, I did relax and arrived at the stage where I was able to go out for walks and enjoy the experience. After a couple of minor mishaps, I arrived at the place where I was ready to take my final test and thankfully I passed to become a qualified guide dog owner.

Around the same time though, my wife's condition deteriorated, and she died on 1 December 2018. My life and that of my family would never be the same again. Sylvia had gone to Heaven to be with her Lord and for that, at least, I was incredibly grateful.

A short while after Sylvia's funeral, I awoke one morning with the very strong sense within me that Eaton needed to be returned to the Guide Dog Centre. I battled with this for a day or two, thinking how disappointing this would be for the trainers who had invested so much time and money in my training, not to mention the effect this may have on Eaton and the loss my family would feel.

I knew, however, after a few days that I had to make this difficult phone call and request that someone come and take Eaton away. If Sylvia had still been with us then I believe so would Eaton, but life was now different. Guide Dogs were very understanding and said that I had done a great job in training Eaton up to become a very good guide dog and that, being the breed he was, he would bond with anyone who showed him a bit of love and fed him. I jokingly replied, "Just like a man then?"

I was given a two-week cooling off period for if I wanted to change my mind, but I knew immediately this was the right decision.

What followed was remarkable. The following day I awoke with the strong sense that God was saying I was to read John 14, 15 and 16 from the Bible and totally immerse myself in it so, over the next few days, that is what I did.

John 14 begins with Jesus preparing his closest friends for his death the following day. He said to them I do not want you to have a troubled heart and that's what he was saying to me. He said, "John, I do not want you to have a troubled and a broken heart over Sylvia. She is now safe with me, but your time is not yet. When your time comes, I will come for you, but do not be overwhelmed by grief because Sylvia is in a good place." Well, that brought me such incredible comfort and still does.

In the days that followed, as I read those three chapters over and over, God led me to think about the many references to the Holy Spirit. Jesus said to his friends that they should not be fearful or anxious because he would send them another comforter or advocate who would be with them. This was speaking of the Holy Spirit and the original meaning of Jesus' words is that he will send someone who comes alongside to help or guide.

As I thought about this, within myself I said, "Oh, like a guide dog". I felt God respond and say "Yes, but you do not need a guide dog, for I will be your guide God". It hit me right between the eyes, or deep down in the heart. God was saying to me that, just as you have had to learn to trust in Eaton as your guide dog, now learn to trust in me as your guide God. God was saying to me that I needed to listen to the inner voice. In the book of Romans, we read that God's Spirit will bear witness with our spirit that we are the sons of God. I had an excited sense that I was beginning a brand-new adventure in learning to walk by faith and listen to my God in a way that I had not done for many years.

It's been a truly amazing year since then as I have sought to cultivate this deeper, more personal relationship with Jesus. Within a couple of weeks, I was faced with another big decision and I was glad that I was listening to the voice of my guide God.

Right out of the blue I received an email inviting me to view a two-bedroom assisted living apartment near to the centre of Solihull. I was not thinking of moving to a new house, but my guide God was urging me not to pass this over but take a look. I did so and together with my kids, we agreed that this new apartment was just perfect for me. So it was that after 30 years I moved out of the family home into where I am now. I have prophetically called it "The Well" because it is where I come every day to drink of the rivers of living water, so that I can give out to others.

Oh, and by the way, The Well, as I have named it, is apartment number 14 and remember God directed me to immerse myself in John 14. I have a friend who now calls me John 14!

I miss the lovely Eaton of course and I miss my beautiful, amazing Sylvia even more, but even in this time of lockdown, I awake each morning as I wait upon my guide God for my daily instructions. Locked in or not, each day is a Fantastic Adventure In Trusting Him (FAITH), so why not invite Jesus to be your guide God and set out on a great adventure with him today.

* * *

17. GUARD GOD

In my previous article, I explained how I had been led to send back my guide dog, Eaton, because I believed that God had spoken into my heart and said "I will be your guide God". Since then, I have been re-learning how to trust in, and be led by, the Holy Spirit.

Recently while in prayer, I sensed God saying, "Now I want to be your guard God" and have since heard at least four stories about dogs, with the last two being specifically about guard dogs. One of my favourite footballers, Jack Grealish, the present captain of Aston Villa, has paid £20,000 to get himself a guard dog following recent break-ins at the homes of wealthy footballers. Clearly this expensive purchase has been motivated by fear, but as Christians, we need have no fear.

As I have been pondering this over the last few days, I am prompted to offer you the following words of encouragement …

As a devoted follower of Jesus Christ, you need not be anxious or afraid, even in these troubled, uncertain times. God is with you at all times, He will never leave or forsake you. As the Psalmist wrote, "No good thing will He withhold from those who walk uprightly". God, the Holy Spirit, is omnipresent and He lives in you. The protecting, healing, delivering and saving blood of Jesus is over you and the mighty Angel of the Lord is encamped around you.

How's that for a guard God! You can live with confidence today in the knowledge that your guard God and your guide God have nothing but good plans for you. "For I know the plans I have for you, says the Lord, for good and not disaster; to give you a future and a hope" (Jeremiah 29:11).

As lockdown restrictions are slowly being lifted, there is a lot of fear around. People are worried that if they go out they will catch the virus. Those feelings are understandable but if you are a follower of Jesus Christ, He wants to assure you of His protection. Just think of, and picture in your mind, what a guard dog looks like. They are highly trained and appear to be somewhat ferocious. In other words, you would not mess with them. In the Bible there are many Scriptures which tell us that God is our protector; our shield; our defender; our fortress and strong tower; plus many more besides.

You can go out with faith, joy and confidence, knowing that El Shaddai (God Almighty) is your guard God.

* * *

18. HIGH-RISE HOWLERS

I thought it was time I posted something a bit more light-hearted to try and put a smile on your face. Early on in our marriage Sylvia and I lived in a high-rise block of flats in Birmingham on the 15th floor. The incidents below are taken from my first book "Fear, Fun and Faith" in which there are many more humorous anecdotes.

Over the Top

I discovered very early on in our marriage that Sylvia is a wonderful housekeeper. She is one of those rare people (I think) who actually loves housework, although she draws the line at ironing; one of her pet hates. As part of her housework routine she would rearrange the furniture quite regularly.

I came home from work one night, breezed in through the living room door and had hardly got my usual "Hello sweetheart" out of my mouth when I went headfirst over the back of the settee. I ended up with my face where my backside should have been, with my legs up in the air behind me. Try it sometime and you will soon get the picture. After that, Sylvia decided that rearranging the furniture with a blind person around was maybe not such a good idea after all.

No Smoke without Fire!

Again, quite early on in our marriage I was sitting down watching television while Sylvia was in the kitchen cooking the tea – something with chips I seem to recall. At one point I could smell the whiff of smoke but thought something had just been overcooked in the kitchen. Wisdom, I thought, said don't interfere as Sylvia will have it all in hand. After a few minutes, however, the smell had definitely intensified so I went off to the kitchen to investigate.

Poking my head tentatively around the kitchen door I said, "Everything okay love, I can smell smoke".

The kitchen was next to the living room, so Sylvia came out and on entering the living room, she yelled "Oh my God, the television's on fire".

Apparently, there was smoke billowing out from the back of it and so she picked it up wholesale, having disconnected it from the mains of course and put it out on to the balcony of our 15th floor council flat.

Once things (or more precisely, Sylvia) had calmed down, she said "Didn't you smell the smoke?"

"Yes" I responded, "but I thought it was coming from the kitchen and I didn't like to interfere while you were cooking".

When I'm Cleaning Windows

That was a good song, wasn't it? By George Formby of course, one of my Mum's all-time favourites. He was one of mine too. I loved his movies going right back to the 1930s and 1940s with what became his very famous catchphrase, "Turned out nice again hasn't it". They were very funny movies with the ukulele-playing George often playing the shy, clumsy individual who always gets the girl in the end. Similar in a way to the great Norman Wisdom who was to come later and even to dear old Michael Crawford playing the hapless Frank Spencer in *Some Mother's Do Have `Em!*

I loved George Formby's songs too though I don't know how he got away with some of those cheeky lyrics way back in those far less permissive days. If you have never sampled George's work, try and get hold of a copy of one of his old movies or even his greatest hits album and give yourself a jolly good laugh. Oh yes, well worthy of inclusion in the Fun section of this book.

Anyway, back to the subject of windows. Whilst living in that same flat, can you imagine what it was like to clean the windows outside when you are 15 floors up in the air? Well it is easy when the windows revolve as these did. The trouble is, as Sylvia discovered, when you are so high up and you revolve such a large pane of glass, it is as though you are being pulled to the ground and you also have the scary thought, "What if the window should drop out and fall to the ground, putting people's lives at risk?" In that situation, therefore, I came in very handy being blind. When it came time to clean the outside of the windows Sylvia would take herself off into another room whilst I revolved the window and cleaned it to the best of my ability. Sylvia would pop back into the room to examine my work and would let me know if I had missed any dirt. Yes, it was all great fun, for me at any rate, because it was one of those rare times when I actually felt as though I was doing something useful around the house, apart from washing up the dishes that is!

Unlucky 13

One final story comes to mind from those days in the flat. Arriving home from work one night I got off the bus which stopped right outside Warstone Tower, Bromford Bridge, where we lived, on the site of the old Birmingham Racecourse. I entered the block of flats and pressed the button for the lift. On entering the lift, I counted the buttons down from the top as that was the quickest way being 15 floors up. When the lift stopped, I got out and turned to the left, through the swing doors and using the handle, I opened the front door to the flat. On entering I walked down the hall towards the living room saying, "Hello love, I'm home", only to be greeted by a hefty sounding Irishman saying "What do you want mate?"

"Oh" I said, "am I in the wrong flat?" now knowing that I was because the smell was different and the carpet under foot was unfamiliar to me. I quickly established that I had actually got off the lift at floor 13 by mistake, so I made my sincere apologies and beat a hasty retreat.

* * *

19. HONOUR GOD AND ONE ANOTHER

The principle of honouring runs throughout the Bible. God says in 1 Samuel 2:30 "The one who honours me, I will also honour". We are also called to honour our mother and father, our national and spiritual leaders and also one another. Honouring brings blessings and the favour of God upon our lives. Here, I want to concentrate on honouring one another.

In the late 1980s the Sunday Mercury ran a centre-page spread on the then Aston Villa Chairman, Doug Ellis.

There were some photographs around Mr Ellis' lounge and the reporter commented on two photographs either side of the fireplace. One was of the Aston Villa team that won the European Cup in 1982 and the other was of the evangelist Billy Graham.

Apparently, Doug met Billy when Mission England took place at Villa Park. They had a conversation together over a meal and Doug, from then on, regarded Billy very highly even to the point of his photograph sharing pride of place in his lounge with his beloved Aston Villa team.

I decided to send the article to the Billy Graham Organisation in London for onward transmission to Billy himself, if they felt it right to do so.

Imagine my delight when about six weeks later I received a handwritten letter from Billy Graham himself, thanking me for my kindness in forwarding the article and to say he had the utmost respect for Doug Ellis and was praying for him daily.

How impressive is that? A man who must have received so many letters, took time out to handwrite a personal reply. That speaks to me of character and integrity and is in stark contrast to the many people who cannot even acknowledge a text or an email. In choosing to respond to me in such a personal way, when he was so famous and busy, Billy Graham honoured me with his letter.

I have written to many people over the years, the famous and the not-so-famous. My intentions have usually been to offer thanks, appreciation and/or encouragement. I was once asked on a radio interview if I receive many replies considering all of the letters I wrote. I replied by saying that the ratio was about one in ten. The interviewer commented that that was not many, but I responded by saying that the one reply encouraged me for ten more.

Over the years I have received personal replies from people such as Brian Clough, Graham Taylor, Tommy Steele, Jimmy Crickett, Boney M and the Duke of Cambridge. In each case I felt honoured to receive the reply and in turn I honour them for their courtesy.

If I have let you down in anyway by not replying to your text, email, letter or voicemail, please forgive me. It was an oversight on my part and not intentional I can assure you, but by God's grace I will do better.

I do believe it is important that if someone has taken the time and trouble to be in touch, by whatever means, we can honour them with some kind of acknowledgement.

One final thing, and I credit my friend Elizabeth for teaching me this, remember the "e" in email stands for encouragement. In fact, when it comes to any form of communication, before you engage and then send it off, make sure your message, in whatever format, contains the ingredient of encouragement. As I have become well-known for saying, "No one ever died from an overdose of encouragement". We all thrive on it, so let's be intentional about extravagantly lavishing it on people. Maybe then we will see more people being raised up to fulfil their potential.

* * *

20. HOW TO FLOW IN THE PURPOSES OF GOD

I believe that God has a purpose for every individual and every local church. *"When David had served God's purpose in his own generation, he fell asleep." Acts 13:36*

You and I are here now and, like David, we can only serve the purpose of God in our own generation. When we have done that then, like David, we will fall asleep. By way of a warning, let's not "fall asleep" spiritually or physically before our time and work is done.

I will never forget the occasion I was invited to preach at a church one morning. It was a "Tear Fund Sunday" designed to raise money and create awareness of that great Christian Charity. I had been invited with the strict instructions to preach the Gospel for 20 minutes.

As part of the service we watched a short film from Tear Fund called "Water" and it was highlighting the Charity's work overseas in creating wells where people were desperate for water.

As I listened, something strange began to happen. I sensed the Holy Spirit speaking to me and telling me I should bring a completely different message and, almost instantaneously, I saw in my mind's eye the five points I was to speak on and they were all taken from each letter of the word water. I struggled within myself, because my clear instructions were to preach the Gospel even if, as I assumed, there were no non-Christians in the building.

When my time came to stand up and preach I found a great boldness and explained to the congregation that God, I believe, had given me this very direct word to encourage the church to move on in the purposes of God.

Now I believe God wants me to share this again in the confident hope that it will encourage and motivate someone reading to get moving again.

Willingness for Change
It's so easy to get stuck in a rut, as that church had done years ago. God is on the move and to journey with Him, each one of us must be willing for change in our lives. If we are truly surrendered to God, then we will be willing to accept whatever He has for us. Do not stagnate, God has so much more for you.

Accept Jesus as Lord and King
As I have shared in a previous posting, it is so easy to glibly declare "Jesus is my Lord", but is he really? Is everything you are, and have, available to God for Him to do whatever He pleases?

Thanksgiving and Praise
Right now, in whatever circumstance you find yourself, are you overflowing with thanksgiving and praise to your God. He is worthy and always will be, whatever your circumstances.

Encourage One Another Every Day
I am well-known by my friends for saying, "No one ever died from an overdose of encouragement". This is so true, and encouragement is so powerful. Many people get discouraged and suffer from low self-esteem, even Christians. I know it only too well. I also know that encouraging words and actions are incredibly powerful and have the ability to transform our lives. Many will know that the encouraging words and actions of one of my senior managers transformed my career after I had been stuck in a rut of my own making for over 20 years. Make it part of your life's mission to encourage people every day and even more so as you see the day of Jesus' return drawing near. (Hebrews 10:25)

Restoration and Revival
Make no mistake, God is on a mission. He is a God of restoration, with a clear plan to restore mankind to its rightful place of ruling and reigning. In the Garden of Eden, Adam was given the authority to rule in the Earth but he surrendered that right to the serpent. Jesus, however, by his sinless life, death, resurrection and ascension has regained that authority and given it to His Church, the Bride. He

has made us now to sit with him in Heavenly places, the place of authority. This is our restoration inheritance, to rule and reign with Jesus our King, but the training ground is now.

In addition, we are to be people of revival. That is not so much crying out to God for an outpouring of the Holy Spirit, good though that is, but is more about personal day by day revival. It's about coming to God each morning and being revived afresh for each new day. "As the deer pants for the water, so my soul longs after you." (Psalms 42:1)

The church where I preached this message did not invite me back for another 25 years, until a new generation of leaders had been raised up. I pray that your response will be more immediate as you determine in your heart to serve the purpose of God in your generation.

* * *

21. HYPOCRITE (Part 1)

It's not very nice when someone calls you a hypocrite is it? Or maybe that's never happened to you. Jesus had a few things to say about the subject, mainly to the Pharisees, of course. By the way, there are still some of that sect still around today; I am sure you will have come across them. Sadly, many of them hang around church!

On a few occasions it has been my experience to be called out by the Holy Spirit. On two occasions I can recall this happening even while I have been preaching.

I was speaking on the Lordship of Jesus and boldly declaring, "If He's not Lord of all, then He's not Lord at all". No sooner had the words come out of my mouth than I sensed within me the word "Hypocrite". Anyone who has done any public speaking, particularly preachers, will tell you it is not just possible, but even probable, that there are times when you will be having a conversation with God on the inside, even while you are preaching.

Continuing to preach on the Lordship of Jesus, I knew the Holy Spirit was putting his finger on two areas of my life: Aston Villa and pop records. Inwardly, to resolve the dispute I promised God I would deal with this as I carried on preaching with, hopefully, nobody in the congregation being aware of my inner turmoil.

Clearly these were two idols in my life that had to be dealt with. At the time I had not missed an Aston Villa home game for many years, and I was very proud of that achievement. I remember telling Sylvia, "I am not going to the Villa again" and then going on to explain why. My friends were shocked when I told them, but I kept to my word and did not go to another Aston Villa game for about four years. Eventually someone offered me a couple of tickets to a home game against West Ham United but I politely refused, explaining the reason why. Sylvia, however, encouraged me to accept the tickets saying, "I think you have learned your lesson now and it will no longer be a god to you".

I did not need much persuading. I accepted the tickets and went to the game with a friend. Villa won the game 4-0 and I really enjoyed it. The great thing was though that when the next match came around, I had no interest in going.

Now as for the pop records, here again I was very proud of my collection of over 700 records comprising of singles and albums. At the time of going blind, those records in particular, brought me so much comfort.

To prove to God that these did not have a total hold over my life I came to the difficult decision to sell half of my collection and, with the money raised, I paid for Sylvia and I and the children to have a holiday in Blackpool.

Shortly after that we hit upon some financial challenges that meant we could not pay our utility bills. I remember bringing these needs to God in prayer, but each time I did I kept on hearing that inner voice saying, "What about selling the rest of your record collection to pay the bills?" This was really uncomfortable and challenging but in the end, to reclaim my peace I did sell them and sure enough was able to pay the bills.

Now the lesson here is that you cannot out-give God and if he is asking you to give up something for Him, it is only because He wants to replace it with something better and more fruitful.

Having laid Aston Villa on the altar, as it were, a few years later God called me to connect with the Club and form the Aston Villa Christian Supporters Association and that has led to me having a long-term relationship with the Club. They know I am a Christian and what I stand for. A couple of years ago, at the End of Season Awards Dinner, they presented me with a trophy, which is the Pride of Aston Villa Award for my many years of positive support of the Club.

Having disposed of all of my original record collection, God then opened up a door for me to promote Christian music for Word Records and I used to receive loads of new releases every month. Also, as I mentioned in a previous article, a wonderful opportunity came my way to review the latest Christian records on BBC WM on Sunday mornings and I did that for nearly 15 years, assisting the presenter Michael Blood.

It's okay to have hobbies, but don't let the hobbies have you. Jesus is not my hobby, He is my life and yes, He is my Lord. Can you say that today, without the Holy Spirit echoing the word "Hypocrite"?

* * *

22. HYPOCRITE (Part 2)

One night I was preaching on the theme of overcoming our fears. My text was taken from Psalm 34:4 "I sought the Lord and he heard me and delivered me from all my fears". I was hardly into the message when I heard that inner voice once again saying "Hypocrite". A similar sort of silent conversation took place as the one I described previously. This time the Holy Spirit was reminding me of my fear of the dentist and the fear of water. It was almost as if the Lord was saying, "Preach it like you believe it and we will deal with these two later".

The truth was, I had a very nasty experience at the school dental clinic when I was about 10 years of age. I was referred by the dental nurse to the clinic to have some teeth out. I honestly cannot remember how many. My Mum took me along and the first thing I can recall, was the nurse trying to fit a gas mask on to me. They also fixed a clamp to my mouth to force it wide open. I felt like my mouth was being stretched uncomfortably wide as I lay back in the chair and then the mask went over my face. The gas smelt awful but in a very short time I was fast asleep in a deep dream. I was being lifted up high into the sky via a hook in my mouth. The higher I ascended the more uncomfortable my mouth became, and it was as if the hook was tearing my face apart.

When I came round there was blood all over my clothes, my face, and my hands. It was truly horrible.

From that moment I never went to the dentist again. Now years later, I was married and had three young children. I would be expecting them to go to the dentist along with Sylvia and after the Holy Spirit had been convicting me, I knew I had to confront my fear and take a lead in this matter.

I duly made an appointment and went to see Mr Frazer. I explained to him about my terrifying experience at the school clinic and that I had not been to the dentist since. Well he proceeded to check my teeth, give them a clean and a polish. Then to my surprise he said that considering I had neglected them for so long, they were okay. I must admit that I had been gripping the chair tightly with eyes closed and imagining Jesus upon the Cross having those nails in his hands and feet. I said to myself "It's no longer I that live but Christ who lives in me" and so the Jesus who took the nails could also take away my fear of the dentist. Well it worked for me and, ever since, I have had no problem in keeping up my regular six-monthly appointment at the dentist.

I had been scared of deep water for as long as I could remember. My sister Joan nearly drowned on holiday when we were small children so whether that had anything to do with it, I don't know. In school I would make any excuse I could to get out of going to the swimming baths; I just hated it so much.

I continued through life not giving it much thought, though on occasions when the children went swimming, I did wish I could join them because they seemed to be having so much fun.

I knew that God had put his finger on this fear, but somehow, I managed to wriggle out of dealing with it. Then one day Sylvia saw in the local newspaper that in Solihull, the Council were starting up a club designed to help people with disabilities to learn to swim. Sylvia read this to me, and I knew that God was saying something like, "Run away from this one if you dare".

Well I knew I could not run away any longer, so I made the phone call and registered to become a member of Solihull Seals.

On my first nerve-racking visit I was introduced to a Dr McKenzie, who would be my instructor. Quite a few people had tried to teach me to swim before then, but I never trusted them in the way I did Dr McKenzie – I knew he would not let me drown!

I do not breathe very well through my nose and as a result I would often get mouthfuls of water. The good doctor, however, inspired confidence in me to the point where one night he gave me a resounding round of applause, saying "That's it you can swim now, you have just swum five metres".

I must admit it did not feel as if I had actually been swimming, but the following week I was presented with my five metres badge, which Sylvia sewed on to my shorts. I think she was almost as proud as I was, and I wore those shorts with some smugness for a few years after that. A hearing problem has prevented me going swimming for a long time now, but at least God made it possible for me to confront and overcome that fear of water.

As you have read this, are there any fears in your life which you would like to invite God to help you overcome? I know He does not want our lives to be blighted in any way by fear.

"I sought the Lord and he heard me and delivered me from all my fears". Psalm 34:4

* * *

23. "JESUS, JESUS, JESUS!"

As a Christian I am not ashamed to say, "I love Jesus". In fact, the Bible declares that we love Him because He first loved us.

Of course, I am also a football (soccer) enthusiast and, as such, I have become aware that there are quite a few players with the name 'Jesus' in the game today. Here in the UK one of our top sides, Manchester City, have a star player from Brazil by the name of Gabriel Jesus. My own Club, Aston Villa, have a Director of Football by the name of Jesus Garcia Pitarch. In fact, the name of Jesus has been popular in the Middle East and Spanish-speaking countries for a great many years.

When Christians gather together for worship, we sing songs such as *There is Power in the Name of Jesus*, *How Sweet the Name of Jesus Sounds*, *Praise the Name of Jesus* and many, many more. In so doing, nowadays, I sometimes find my mind turning to the Jesus' I know through my love of football, or even the coach driver I had on my Spanish holiday a few years ago.

I know that sports stars, like pop singers, movie stars etc are worshipped by their fans almost as gods, but the Jesus I am referring to is totally unique. In fact, to give him his full name and title, which I believe we should, he is The Lord Jesus Christ. The title "Lord" means that this Jesus wants to rule and reign in our lives and the word "Christ" means The Anointed One and the Bible reveals to us in the passage below, "There is no other name under Heaven, given by men, by which we must be saved". Let there be no doubt in your mind, no other Jesus, however good they are, can save you, transform you and give you everlasting life.

I invite you to read about that for yourself in this story about Peter and John. The friends of Jesus were being held to account because they dared to heal a man who had been lame from birth.

Acts 4 (The Message Bible)

While Peter and John were addressing the people, the priests, the chief of the Temple police, and some Sadducees came up, indignant that these upstart apostles were instructing the people and proclaiming that the resurrection from the dead had taken place in Jesus. They arrested them and threw them in jail until morning, for by now it was late in the evening. But many of those who listened had already believed the Message—in round numbers about five thousand!
The next day a meeting was called in Jerusalem. The rulers, religious leaders, religion scholars, Annas the Chief Priest, Caiaphas, John, Alexander—everybody who was anybody was there. They stood Peter and John in the middle of the room and grilled them: "Who put you in charge here? What business do you have doing this?"
With that, Peter, full of the Holy Spirit, let loose: "Rulers and leaders of the people, if we have been brought to trial today for helping a sick man, put under investigation regarding this healing, I'll be completely frank with you—we have nothing to hide. By the name of Jesus Christ of Nazareth, the One you killed on a cross, the One God raised from the dead, by means of his name this man stands before you healthy and whole. Jesus is 'the stone you masons threw out, which is now the cornerstone.' Salvation comes no other way;

no other name has been or will be given to us by which we can be saved, only this one."
They couldn't take their eyes off them—Peter and John standing there so confident, so sure of themselves! Their fascination deepened when they realized these two were laymen with no training in Scripture or formal education. They recognized them as companions of Jesus, but with the man right before them, seeing him standing there so upright—so healed!—what could they say against that?
They sent them out of the room so they could work out a plan. They talked it over: "What can we do with these men? By now it's known all over town that a miracle has occurred, and that they are behind it. There is no way we can refute that. But so that it doesn't go any further, let's silence them with threats so they won't dare to use Jesus' name ever again with anyone."
They called them back and warned them that they were on no account ever again to speak or teach in the name of Jesus. But Peter and John spoke right back, "Whether it's right in God's eyes to listen to you rather than to God, you decide. As for us, there's no question—we can't keep quiet about what we've seen and heard."

In the same way, I can't keep quiet about what I have seen and heard!

* * *

24. JESUS THE SUPER-SUB

Those of us who love sport, could be excused for having withdrawal symptoms at the moment. Almost two months without football, let alone rugby and the other sports that take up so much of our time. It's now the cricket season too and more often than not, for the first few County Championship matches we have to endure cold winds and rain; even snow cannot be ruled out. The sunshine of recent weeks though has been a great blessing to the millions of us who are in lockdown, locked in and locked up because of the coronavirus.

I am missing my football fix though. I must be a Masochist, being an Aston Villa supporter!!

One of the quirks of football is how a player can come on as a substitute with relatively little time left in the game and almost single-handedly transform the score-line. These individuals are often called "impact" players because they have the effect of giving the spectators a big lift, thus raising the atmosphere and volume levels. They also inspire their teammates. Very often this player who has been watching the game from the sidelines and weighing up the opposition, comes off the bench then almost immediately scores a vital goal.

The scenario described above reminds me so vividly of Jesus Christ, because the Bible teaches me that he became my substitute when he went to the Cross. In the game of life, which every one of us is involved in, God saw that we weren't doing at all well ("All we like sheep have gone astray and gone each one to our own way …") and that without his intervention we would all die without hope. So it was that Jesus (God's very own Son) came to Earth, lived a sinless life, died upon the Cross as the Saviour of the world, rose again from the dead and now lives for evermore.

Jesus, totally victorious in every area of life and death is ready and willing to come into our lives if we will only surrender to Him.

Why not invite Him to come off the proverbial bench, enter into your life and he will be your glorious substitute in everything pertaining to life and death.

Once Jesus is active in your life, a quick look at the end of the Bible will show you that you are on the victory side. Death, your ultimate enemy, is defeated and you are raised up to everlasting life with Jesus.

What a substitute! Definitely a "Man of the Match" performance!

* * *

25. KEEP ON DRINKING

Social distancing is something we hear about all the time these days, but social drinking too is massive in many cultures, including our own. Binge drinking has become a big problem in many countries, especially at weekends, as people want to go out, get drunk and have a jolly good time.

Yesterday I went for a walk alongside a friend (of a certain vintage!) and as we passed by a pub, which was shut of course, he jokingly said, "Shall we pop in for a swift half?". Now that's a phrase people of my parents' generation used to use quite often. In fact, my Dad said it every time he took me to an Aston Villa match when I was a child. He would leave me outside the pub with other children, drinking lemonade and eating a bag of crisps. Unfortunately, Dad's "swift half" I think turned into two or three, given the time I was left impatiently waiting.

Sadly, I think it's the case that a great many Christians are satisfied with a "swift half" when it comes to being filled with the Holy Spirit. The desire that people have to drink alcohol heavily and lose their inhibitions so they can have a good time, is not so far removed from what God wants for us. Just take a look in Acts 2 on the day of Pentecost when the 120 believers gathered in that upper room. The Holy Spirit came upon them and they were filled to overflowing with joy and gladness, not to mention supernatural power.

The crowds who gathered to find out what the commotion was all about, actually accused them of being drunk, but they were overflowing (drunk) with the Holy Spirit. In Ephesians 5 we are told to go on day by day being filled with the Holy Spirit so we may overflow with psalms, hymns, spiritual songs etc. In real terms (as the Politicians say), from God's perspective, a swift half is not good enough. We need to be, as we read in Psalm 42:1 "As the deer pants for the water, so my soul pants after you". Jesus said, "Blessed are those who hunger and thirst after his righteousness, for they shall be filled".

God is more keen to fill you to overflowing than many of us are to be filled. I heard a preacher once reverently say, "Never ask God to pour you a cup of tea, because he never knows when to stop and it would overflow everywhere into the saucer and on to the table". Are you getting the message? God wants us to overflow so that we bless the world around us.

For the last couple of years, I have developed, what one doctor called, "Dry Mouth Syndrome". I have had various tests, but no reason can be found for this. The doctor just said to me, "Keep on drinking lots of water". It's a bit embarrassing as a public speaker when you have a dry mouth, but as I keep on drinking, it serves as a great reminder to me as to the spiritual need to keep on drinking.

A lot is said today about the dangers of becoming dehydrated and that is particularly the case as we grow older. The experts, therefore, tell us to drink more and more water, so as to stay hydrated and healthy. Are you a dehydrated Christian today and feeling very dry? The remedy is simple, come and take a drink. In John 7 Jesus cried out with a loud voice, "Is anyone thirsty?" Today Jesus is wanting to get your attention and invite you to come afresh to those rivers of living water and drink deeply of him. He wants to revive and refresh you, equipping you for the next exciting stage of life.

During this pandemic the pubs maybe shut, but The King's Arms are open, and you are invited in for a drink, so come on in and keep on drinking!

* * *

26. KEEP THE HOME FIRE BURNING!

The title of this article is taken from one of the most famous songs of World War I and was later popularized in at least three films. The song is sung by Joan Fontaine and a group of British soldiers in the 1942 film *This Above All*. It was then included in the 1969 musical *Oh What a Lovely War* and in the 1970 musical film *Darling Lili*.

With this thought in mind, let's take a look at the following passage of Scripture:

Leviticus 6: 8-13 (New International Version)

The Burnt Offering

The LORD said to Moses: Give Aaron and his sons this command: 'These are the regulations for the burnt offering: The burnt offering is to remain on the altar hearth throughout the night, till morning, and the fire must be kept burning on the altar. The priest shall then put on his linen clothes, with linen undergarments next to his body, and shall remove the ashes of the burnt offering that the fire has consumed on the altar and place them beside the altar. Then he is to take off these clothes and put on others, and carry the ashes outside the camp to a place that is ceremonially clean. The fire on the altar must be kept burning; it must not go out. Every morning the priest is to add firewood and arrange the burnt offering on the fire and burn the fat of the fellowship offerings on it. The fire must be kept burning on the altar continuously; it must not go out."

Despite the fact that most of our homes now enjoy the benefits of central heating, there are still many who enjoy an old-fashioned log or coal fire roaring away on a cold winter's night. Admittedly, they do look great and give out a great deal of warmth. First of all, of course, it takes time to build the fire and secondly next morning someone has to get down on their hands and knees and remove the ashes before building a fresh fire.

Spiritually that is exactly the same for us. In the short Bible passage, we read that the ashes had to be removed and taken outside the city. This reminds me that, at the start of each new day, we have to remove the ashes of yesterday. This is a new day and whatever went on yesterday is now passed into history. We have to forget the good, the bad and the ugly, as it were, remove them from our thinking and build a fresh fire every day. Personally, I build a fresh fire by beginning with words of thanksgiving, adoration, worship and praise.

God's command is that we remove the ashes and that the fire MUST burn continually; it MUST not go out. In 1 Thessalonians 5 Paul writes, "Do not put out the Spirit's fire". Sometimes I fall into the trap of asking God to light my fire and, though He understands my heart, the responsibility lies with me and you to fan the fire into flame every day. The Father is looking for a heart that's ablaze with gratitude and appreciation for who He is and for all that He has done.

When John Wesley encountered the Holy Spirit, he said that his heart was strangely warmed. I pray that in reading this short article your heart will be warmed, if it's grown cold, or heated up even more as you obey God and Keep the Home Fire Burning.

* * *

27. LAUNCH OUT INTO THE DEEP (Part 1)

In Luke's Gospel, chapter 5, we read the story of Jesus walking on the beach and seeing some of his friends looking tired and dispirited. They were fishermen and they have been out on their boats all night and caught nothing. Jesus (a carpenter, remember) then says to Peter, "Launch out into the deep and lower your nets for a great catch". Well I can imagine the look of disbelief and anger on Peter's face, but thankfully he responded by saying, "Although we have toiled all night, at your word, we will". Of course, they ended up with the most amazing catch of fish and their nets almost bursting.

I will never forget the time God burned this phrase, "Launch out into the deep" in my heart.

Sylvia and I were working on a council housing estate in Birmingham. We hosted a meeting called "One Way Special" on Monday nights in our home for children aged between 5 and 12. On Fridays we held a youth group and I also delivered a Christian newspaper to about 200 homes every month. Shortly after, Beverley, our first child was born, it seemed like everywhere we went that Scripture was being preached.

We heard it in church meetings, in our daily bible-reading notes and even on the radio. Launch out into the deep was screaming at us and soon it became clear that what God was saying was that I should give up my job in the Civil Service, continue the work on the housing estate and totally trust him for our finances. That really was launching out into the deep and it took me six months to pluck up the courage to act on that word. At the office, my bosses were so concerned for me, they said they would keep my job open for a month.

I remember that what most scared me was how I would pay the rent for our council property. We need not have worried: a few days before my one-month notice period was up, we received a letter from the council to say that for some reason I had neglected to claim a rent rebate to which we had been entitled and so our rent for the remainder of the financial year would be 48 pence per week, rising to 98 pence per week the following year. That was so exciting because I thought, we could just about have faith for that. From then on it was a case of learning to trust God in every situation. Sometimes we got it right and sometimes we got it wrong, but it was certainly an adventure for a few years.

I now realise that the words "Launch out into the deep", for me at least were not just for then, but they are to be my lifestyle. We were never meant to drop anchor and settle for a comfort zone but, as believers, we are designed to have a life of continually launching out with the aim of reaching people.

One night I was in a house group meeting and I plucked up the courage to sing out a new song in tongues. As I was doing so, I sensed the Holy Spirit urging me to sing it again in English. This was a real matter of trust on my part, but the words which came out were as follows:

"I want to do something crazy
I want to do something good.
I want to do something crazy for you, Lord.
To love you, to trust you, to depend upon your Word
I want to do something crazy for you, Lord."

There were two people in the room who had been praying about buying a house, but they thought it was a bit crazy as it was more than they could really afford. They took the word by faith, did it and God prospered them.

The Bible is laden with stories of people who did apparently crazy things. Just look at people like Noah, Abraham, Gideon, David and so on, let alone Jesus himself.

In the following article, I will tell you about some of the crazy things God (or was it me being impulsive?) has led me into.

For now, though, let me tell you about Arthur Blessitt, someone who has been a great influence on my life and now a friend. In 1968 he was preaching to the hippies in Sunset Boulevard when God told him to build a 12-foot cross and carry it around America. He was obedient to that call but, along the way he sensed God saying to carry the cross to the entire world. Arthur achieved his goal a few years ago and is now in the Guinness Book of Records for being the human being who has done the longest walk in history. In so doing he has brought healing and salvation to hundreds of thousands of people. Now in his 70s, Arthur and his wife Denise are still carrying the cross. How crazy is that then?

This is no time to retire to the country, but re-fire, launch out into the deep and do something crazy for God.

* * *

28. LAUNCH OUT INTO THE DEEP (Part 2)

"The wind blows where it wishes, you can hear its sound, but you do not know where it comes from or where it is going to, so is everyone who is born of the Spirit." Jesus spoke these words to Nicodemus in John 3:8. I call this the glorious unpredictability of being a Christian. Living for Jesus removes the humdrum and the mundane to a large extent, because you just never know what God is going to say to you or where he will lead you.

In my previous article, as part of launching out into the deep, I wrote about how God will often require that we do something which appears crazy to the casual observer. You only have to look at people such as Moses, Abraham, and Gideon, let alone Paul, the crazy adventurer apostle.

One time I was recovering in hospital after an exploratory operation on my left ear, when my attention was aroused by a fascinating interview on the radio. It was with Arthur Blessitt, the man I mentioned previously, who was carrying a 12-foot cross throughout the UK and was appearing in Birmingham that night. Arthur would be preaching in the Bullring and I knew instinctively I had to be there to listen to him. I did something I have never done before or since and signed myself out of hospital. I went with Sylvia and stood with thousands of people to listen to this man from America on a cold winter's night. To open the proceedings, a Gospel group called 11.59 sang a few songs and they were very good. When Arthur spoke though I was enthralled and captivated by his down to earth passion for Jesus. He made being a Christian sound so much fun. Arthur's passion for Jesus and his love for people without question rubbed off and impacted on my life.

At the end, while people were dispersing, I said to Sylvia that I needed to go up and speak with a member of the 11.59 group. I wanted to invite them to come and sing at the youth meeting we ran on the housing estate. That was me being crazy again. I did not stop to think where did the group come from, or how much they may cost.

They gave me their contact details and after writing to them they agreed to come along. There were four members of the group, they travelled up from Oxford, did a concert for us, did not ask for any money (though we gave them some) and they slept on our lounge floor!

Not too long after that, one of our national newspapers ran a double page spread on the rising popularity of the occult in Britain and they gave a list of some of the most popular books on the subject. At our One Way Special children's meetings we became aware that a lot of the childrens' families dabbled in seances, witchcraft and suchlike. We had just read a best-selling book called *From Witchcraft to Christ* which told the true story of Doreen Irvine, who had become a prominent witch and then converted to following Jesus. In the book she warned about the dangers of becoming involved in the occult.

In another crazy move, I made efforts to contact Doreen and invite her to come and speak to the children. I managed to find an address for Doreen in Bristol and so I wrote a letter of invitation to her. Many people were not surprised when I did not get a reply because rumours were afoot that she had gone back into witchcraft. I found this sad and did not want to believe it.

After about a year, I received a letter from America and it was from Doreen. She apologized for the delay but said she had been speaking across America for many months and had only recently seen my letter. Doreen told me that she was coming back to the UK and would be delighted to come and work with us anyway she could. I ended up booking her for 10 days and she spoke at churches, schools, prisons took part in an incredible two-hour phone in on a local radio station, and was also interviewed for our local newspaper. It was a most memorable time.

Coming right up to date, it was rather crazy, on the face of it, to even consider selling up my family home for 30 years, just over one month after Sylvia had died. I knew that the wind of God's Spirit was blowing though, and I got to move into a wonderful apartment that is as though it was tailor-made for me. I prophetically call it, "The Well" because it is from here that I drink from the rivers of living water and so do many who come to visit me.

Are you ready then to launch out into the deep and, as the wind of the Holy Spirit blows afresh on you, do something crazy for God? I know I am.

Enjoying the sun with Sylvia in Cyprus

My first answered prayer - Sylvia!

Outside our home, age 19, learning to walk with my white stick

Manor House Torquay 1969, age 19, training to live as a blind person

Daisy and Oscar - both born on what would have been Sylvia's 70th birthday

Renewal, Solihull - my home church

I just love sharing my faith!

Receiving my MBE at Buckingham Palace in 2015

Pride of Aston Villa Award 2018 for my long-time support of the Club. Presented by Ian Taylor

Sylvia's bench: Located at the entrance to Elmdon Park, Solihull, by St Nicholas' Church. It is a short distance from the car park, about 30m down the path and over to the left by the trees, looking down the hill.

The wording on the plaque - Sylvia's bench

Eaton - my guide dog for a short season

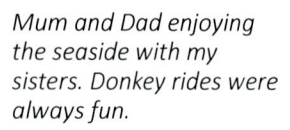

Mum and Dad enjoying the seaside with my sisters. Donkey rides were always fun.

THE WELL - the sign on my appartment door

My dad, Frank Flanner - a Manager at Dunlop Tyres Birmingham

Speaking to a class at Malvern Hall School, Solihull

Come on Villa!

Presenting on BBC Radio Plymouth 1989

Being interviewed on Radio WM

* * *

29. LOCAL CHURCH – THE BENEFITS OF BELONGING

"Let us not forsake meeting together, as is the habit of some, but let us encourage one another everyday as we see the return of Jesus drawing near." (Hebrews 10:25)

Since my beautiful, amazing wife Sylvia became seriously ill and her subsequent departure for Heaven, just over a year ago, I have had cause on many occasions to thank God that I belong to a thriving and highly supportive local church. The advantages of this to me as an individual have been enormous in helping me to deal with my grief in a healthy way and maintain an attitude of thanksgiving.

Below I have listed just a few of the many blessings that are available to me as a committed partner in my local church.

1. I have the opportunity to join with many others in bringing praise and worship to the God I love.

2. I am able to grow in faith and learn more about God and his purposes for my life and the world as I listen to brilliant teaching from the Bible, set in the context of today's world.

3. I have the privilege of being able to contribute financially into the work of God, locally, nationally and internationally.

4. I have so many amazing friends and I feel rich, beyond measure.

5. When challenges and issues come my way, I have access to many resources and skills within the church.

6. I meet with small groups for mutual encouragement, prayer and to 'do life' together.

7. I get to find out my reason for being here, discover and use my talents accordingly.

God always intended that we live in community, not isolated or alone. It is an incredible thrill and privilege to belong to the local church to serve and be served, to love and be loved and to be blessed so I can bless others in return. I am convinced there is no greater joy on the planet than the thrill of belonging to the family of God.

May I urge you, therefore, don't hang loose, get connected and grow in your calling.

* * *

30. MY FATHER LOVES ME

On 8 June 1967, a timid, 19-year-old young man stepped on to a train at Birmingham New Street station with his worried father, bound for Torquay. That was me of course, recently registered blind and heading off for three months' rehabilitation at the Manor House in what is sometimes called "The English Riviera". Believe me I was scared! This was my first time away from home and I had no idea what I was letting myself in for and not being able to see; it felt like a nightmare.

I think Dad and I sat in silence for most of the journey and we took a taxi from Torquay Railway Station up to the Manor House. It was a magnificent old building with wooden floors and a great central staircase. After registering at reception, Dad and I were escorted to the room on the first floor, which would be my home for the next 12 weeks. I would be sharing a room with three older men. One of them I met immediately. He was a cheerful, 40-something-year-old from Lowton in Essex; his name was Les and my Dad spoke with him and asked him to look after me. I am glad to say that Les and I became great friends and he did keep a fatherly eye on me all the time I was at Torquay.

In the evening there was a barn dance to welcome the newcomers, along with a fish and chip supper. It was a pleasant time during which Dad and I were introduced to a few people. At about 10.30pm Dad tapped me on the arm and said, "I think I had better go now and check in at my hotel".

I cannot remember what my reply was, but I took Dad's arm as we walked back together to the reception area. It was an awkward moment preparing to say goodbye, so I reached out to shake Dad's hand. Suddenly, however, he pulled me to him and embraced me tightly and as he did so I could feel his body trembling. Dad began to sob, and his tears drenched my face as he repeated several times, "I am really sorry, son". We held each other tight and wept together. Little did Dad know that he would repeat this scenario two more times, because later Paul, my brother and sister Joan would also go blind. In that moment of embrace, trembling and tears, however, I received a revelation "My father loves me".

Until then, I don't remember love being expressed openly in the family like that. Dad got me a job when I left school, he took us on family holidays to Blackpool and we went to football matches together. Love was clearly present in action, but not expressed in words so much. Once Dad had left me at Torquay, I determined to make a success of the course so that Mum and Dad could be really proud of me and not worry so much.

I very much enjoyed that summer. The course went really well, I made some great friends and developed some new skills. The weather was fabulous too as was the music in what became known as "The summer of love".

On leaving Torquay, having been informed that I had been awarded a place on a course in London to become an audio typist, I returned home for four months. It was on 1 January 1968 that I left home again, this time on my own and far more confident, making my way to Pembridge Place in the Bayswater area of London. This is where I would spend my next eight months and ultimately, where I would discover "my Father loves me all over again".

I loved typing right from the outset, learning to have a smooth rhythm as we typed to the music of Jimmy Shand and his band. Mrs Molly Craig was my teacher and I am indebted to her, not only for getting me up to a high standard so I could pass my exams, but more importantly because she introduced me to Jesus and the concept of being "Born Again".

It was because of Mrs Craig that I found myself at Westminster Chapel one night. Having not been to church for many years, I was nervous and fearful of the unknown. The service was so inspiring; I loved the hymns (ones I knew from school assembly days) and the preacher was interesting to listen to. At the end of the service, I chatted over coffee with someone and in answer to my questions, he explained how I could know God in a personal way. He led me in a prayer, which I repeated after him, thanking God for his love expressed on the cross by Jesus and then surrendering my life to Him. Immediately I was surrounded by people shaking my hand and giving me hugs. It was not long before the revelation hit me, "God really loves me".

For the second time in less than two years, I had felt the warm embrace of a Father's love and it is something I have never forgotten. My earthly father resumed attending church at the age of 80 and received Jesus as his Saviour shortly afterwards. He died at the age of 86 and would have experienced the warm embrace of his Heavenly Father.

I trust you are able to say with me, "My Father loves me".

**

31. MY FIRST ANSWERED PRAYER

In my previous article, I explained how I became a Christian on my one-and-only visit to the iconic Westminster Chapel. Following that service and my life-transforming decision to follow Jesus, I was on a high and wanted to tell everyone about my experience. Not bad for someone who was so desperately shy!

The trouble was that my story was met by family and friends alike, with a great deal of hilarity, cynicism and even fear on the part of my family, as they wondered what on earth I had got myself into. With so much negativity surrounding me, I decided they must be right and that on the night in question at Westminster Chapel I was probably swept along on a wave of emotion.

A week or two later though, I was travelling from London to Birmingham by coach and my head was full of anxiety as many questions ran through my brain. As I thought back to the night at Westminster Chapel, I desperately wanted it to be true. I came away from there with such incredible peace and joy. On the coach, however I had so many questions going around my mind about the existence of God, how to get to Heaven, or even if Heaven existed at all. In the midst of the turmoil, came an idea.

"I am going to pray," I thought, and this is the prayer that came to my mind and I prayed it under my breath as I did not want to disturb the person sitting next to me.

"Dear God, if what happened to me at Westminster Chapel was real, would you please prove it to me by giving me a girlfriend?"

That done, I was immediately filled with a sense of calm. I was 21 years of age and never had a girlfriend, because I was too shy and afraid of rejection to ever ask a girl for a date.

About two weeks later I was back in Birmingham (in those days I was living and working in London because I had just got my first audio typing job with what was then called the Ministry of Overseas Development). It was a Saturday night and my friend Graham and I decided to go to a local pub as we did not have enough money to go to The Heartbeat disco in Birmingham City Centre, which was our normal haunt. My Mum and Dad were at the pub and they were sat round a big table, so Graham and I sat either side of them. A short while later, my sister Joan arrived along with a friend of hers from work and they sat down next to me.

I was just into my first pint of beer when my Dad told me that the man had arrived who was selling cockles and mussels. Eagerly I purchased a bag of cockles and asked Joan's friend, sitting next to me, if she would like a cockle, but she politely refused, and we did not say another word until very much later.

At about 11 o'clock, Dad did what was fairly normal for him, and he invited a few people back to the house for a party. I hated parties, because, parties meant dancing and dancing meant girls and I was scared of girls, remember!

Back at the house I did my usual thing and sat in the corner of the room near my record player. I had several hundred single records and on many of them I had the record sleeves brailled so I knew what I was playing. Yes, you could say I was the disc jockey for the evening. Joan came over to me and said, "Would you play a song for my friend Sylvia because she is going through a really tough time in her life?"

"You mean the one who refused my cockle?" I said somewhat incredulously.

Joan confirmed that it was the same person. So, what I did was to take the first record off the top of the pile, read the braille and boldly announced (because I had downed a few beers by then!) "Ladies and gentlemen, especially for Sylvia, I am playing Mr Pitiful by Otis Reading".

Now I was in for a shock. That same Sylvia came over to me and said, "Thank you for playing that song, it is one of my favourites".

Then as she took me by the hand and pulled me up, she said, "Dance with me?"

I really did not have much choice in the matter, without creating a scene. I felt most uncomfortable to begin with but, very quickly, the realization hit me that I was actually slow dancing with a real live woman. It felt good and I felt so proud that she had asked me. As Otis drew to a close, she returned me to my seat.

I felt great and next day I think I floated back to London.

On the Monday night I received a phone call from Joan saying that I had made a big hit with someone over the weekend and she had a letter to read over the phone to me. Unbelievably it was from Sylvia, who said she liked meeting me and she enjoyed my company. Sylvia said she felt I was the kind of person she could talk with and next time I was in Birmingham, could we meet up. Not one to keep a woman waiting, I was back the following Friday night and Sylvia met me off the coach.

We got on like the proverbial house on fire and the following week I was back again, and we spent all weekend chatting together.

We first met on Saturday 28 December and four weeks later, on Saturday 25 January we were at the aforementioned Heartbeat Club, whilst a most "romantic" record was playing (*Obladi Oblada* by Marmalade) I looked over my rum and coke, into Sylvia's eyes and said, "Sylvia, will you marry me?"

I think she was taken aback for a moment or two because there was silence before she said, "Of course I will".

It's funny because as Sylvia was at the bar getting the drinks, it occurred to me that I had prayed that heartfelt prayer on the coach, God had answered it so why keep him waiting, or Sylvia for that matter.

As I said recently, God knows what he's doing, and Sylvia was the perfect wife for me. I miss her so much now, but I am so grateful to God that we had 50 years together and she is now safe with Jesus enjoying her eternal rewards.

So, the question remains, can you remember your first answered prayer?

* * *

32. MY HEART OVERFLOWS (Psalm 45:1)

What a mighty, wonderful, and amazing God we serve. Some people could, and maybe do, look at my life externally and feel sorry for me. After all Sylvia, my darling wife for 49 years, died 18 months ago, I am blind, have a major hearing impairment and have been in total lockdown for over nine weeks. For all that though, I am as happy, or blessed, as the Bible puts it as any man can be.

In February of last year, I was presented with a golden opportunity to move into a luxurious two bedroom assisted-living apartment, where all of my meals are provided for me, as and when required. Moving house so soon after my wife's death, went against all good counselling advice, but I knew this was God's provision and so did my family.

I had only been in my new place for a short time when I sensed that I should prophetically name my apartment "The Well". One of my kids actually got a plaque made for me that is now on my front door to let everyone know they are entering "The Well".

This apartment has become a place of incredible refreshing not just for me, but for all who visit me, including the church home group, which I host.

Where my apartment is located in the building is perfect for me. I am right on the end on the first floor; I have nobody either side of me and nobody above or below me because I am over an archway. This means I can play my music as loud as I like without disturbing anyone and, even more to the point, I can pray and praise as noisily as I wish. I have total freedom to worship God without any restraint or interruption whatsoever, apart from the telephone that is.

God has also provided me with new friends to stand with me in prayer and those who read to me. In recent times, thanks to them I have been able to listen to brilliant books on the lives of John G Lake, William Booth, Rees Howells, Hudson Taylor and George Muller. I cannot tell you what a blessing this has been to me. When Sylvia was alive and well, she read many books to me over the years, but now God has provided me with other friends to nourish my spirit in this way.

It's in the areas of worship and praise though where God has been taking me on a journey. As I have come to the well each morning to drink of those rivers of living water, I have opened my mouth and my heart has overflowed with new songs of adoration to God. Some of these have been in English and others in tongues. To some I have sung the interpretation, whilst others have been love-songs from me to Jesus. I have been led to sing over myself, over my family, over friends and over the nations.

A few days ago, I sang a new melody and just repeated the words El Shaddai over and over again for half an hour. Of course, those words have a few translations, but mainly they mean "God all mighty" or "The God who is more than enough". A quick look in the book of Revelation shows us that the Angels in Heaven are constantly singing their refrains of worship and praise and they do it non-stop. There can be awesome power in singing a God-given refrain over and over again.

My experience of being a single person in lockdown has shown me just how privileged I am to be able to lavish worship on my God in a totally uninhibited way. My front door is locked, and I have no fear of someone walking in on me. No wonder Jesus said, "When you pray go into your closet and shut the door". When we are alone with God it is such an amazing place to be. Locked in with the creator of all things and the lover of my soul, what an incredible privilege.

I also know that in terms of experiencing worship, praise, adoration and rejoicing as they know it in Heaven, we have only scratched the surface. God is calling us to go much deeper, there are vast rivers out there for us to revel in. It's not just for the trained musicians and singers, but this is available for every believer. Jesus said, "Is anyone thirsty... come to the river and drink and out of your belly (the deepest part of you) will flow those rivers of living water".

Those of us who are "on our own" have an advantage over those who are married and have children running around, because they find it difficult to get times of quiet to be alone with God. Whatever your situation though, it's time to sing a new song to the Lord until your heart overflows and your tongue becomes the pen of a ready writer (Psalm 45:1).

By the way, Sylvia is with Jesus now, having a ball I guess, so that's another reason for my heart to overflow with praise.

* * *

33. NO MORE SAD SONGS

This morning at my church, Renewal Solihull [renewalcc.com] we enjoyed a fantastic on-line service with some great worship and a most uplifting message from our Senior Pastor, Jonny Lee. It was a message that totally resonated within my heart and was in line with some of my recent postings.

"No More Sad Songs", what a great title for our times.

Do you remember when the iPod first came out and other similar music-playing devices? I could hardly get my head around this, thousands of songs on one tiny gadget. This was music to my ears (pun intended). As a teenager I thought the height of luxury would be to own my own juke box, where I could play music at the push of a button. Now I am in music heaven because my precious Alexa, can play millions of songs at the very sound of my voice.

Anyway, going back to the iPod for a moment, I remember the

day when I was marveling about this invention when I sensed the Holy Spirit speak to me and say, "Did you not realise that I have put something deep in your spirit, like an iPod, that has absolutely limitless songs and melodies; some old, some new and some not even written yet, but you will compose them." This was a thrilling revelation, especially for me a non-musician and one not known for a sweet singing voice; I am being kind to myself there.

Since living in my present apartment, where I am ideally located with no one above me, no one below me and no one either side of me, I have been able to give full expression and allow these songs old and new to emerge.

I am able to sing songs of thanksgiving, songs of praise, songs of joy, songs of healing, songs of deliverance, songs of victory, songs of celebration, songs of the age to come etc. Some of these songs have been written by others and can span hundreds of years, such as *Amazing Grace*. Other songs I have never heard before, they have simply risen up out of my spirit. Some are even pop songs, but from my heart they express love to Jesus.

In the book of Proverbs in the Bible we are instructed to guard our hearts with all diligence, because out of it WILL FLOW the issues of life. Then one day Jesus (John 7) cried out with a very loud voice "Is anyone thirsty?" He followed that up by saying if so, then come drink and out of your belly (innermost being) WILL FLOW rivers of living water. The Apostle Paul in Ephesians 5 encourages us not to be filled with wine, but be filled and filled and filled with the Holy Spirit, speaking to one another with psalms, hymns and spiritual songs, with thanksgiving, making melody in our hearts (iPod) to the King of Kings.

So, as Jonny said today "No More Sad Songs". God is either leading us out or he is leading us home. Either way, it's a win-win situation so keep on singing!

If Paul and Silas from the depths of their cold and filthy prison cell, bleeding from the flogging they had experienced simply because they preached good news, could sing praises to God at midnight, then you and I can do it from the comfort of our own homes.

Now come on Alexa, you and I are gonna make some noise as we rejoice together in God's presence!

* * *

34. O WHAT A NIGHT!

I want to tell you about one of the most amazing and life-changing nights of my life. It all took place on Thursday 10 February 1972, on a day which, up until then, had been quite normal. A bit like those shepherds long ago, abiding in the fields keeping watch over their flocks by night, then God broke in and things were never the same again.

Life had been anything but dull leading up to this eventful night. I had been a Christian for just over three years, met and married Sylvia, had our first child Beverley and Sylvia was pregnant with twins, though she didn't know it at the time. Now, just like those shepherds, something was about to happen that would impact my life forever.

Once the baby-sitter had arrived, Sylvia and I set off for the prayer meeting at Kingstanding Elim Church in Birmingham; three days later we were going to be baptized together in the big tank at the same church. The meeting would have started with a few lively praise songs before Pastor Morrison stood up to speak. He described Jesus' disciples following his death, resurrection, and ascension into heaven. I remember him saying that the followers of Jesus were running scared, terrified for their lives in case they too were caught and executed. He went on to say that there are many frightened Christians in the world today and some were in that room, too nervous to speak up for Jesus in the family, the workplace, or in their social circle. I began to fidget in my seat because I could identify with that fear. When I first became a Christian, I had received so much ridicule that I withdrew into my shell.

Pastor Morrison continued by explaining that Jesus, just before He ascended into Heaven, told his followers to go and wait in Jerusalem until He sent the Holy Spirit to be with them. As a result, 120 of them, including the mother of Jesus, were waiting behind locked doors in an upper room. Then suddenly there was the sound of a mighty rushing wind that shook the place in which they were staying, and tongues of fire came and rested upon each one of them. With that they ran out into the streets, everyone speaking with a new earthly and Heavenly language.

From that time on they preached with great boldness and without fear, performing many amazing miracles in the name of Jesus. Subsequently all but one of the Apostles were martyred for their faith, but the point was, they were transformed by the power of the Holy Spirit because they were so convinced of what they had seen and experienced.

Pastor Morrison went on to explain that Jesus had said to his followers, "You will receive dynamite-like power when the Holy Spirit comes upon you and you will become my witnesses to the ends of the Earth". (Acts 1:8) The Pastor further explained that the same power was still available today for all who identified with those early disciples and wanted to be rid of their fears, so they could stand up boldly for Jesus. He invited those people to come forward to receive the laying on of hands to receive, what he called the Baptism in the Holy Spirit.

I immediately left my seat, as did Sylvia, and we stood at the front of the room alongside about a dozen others. Everyone present, maybe about 50 people, were encouraged to begin singing and praising God. Some of the church leaders came along the line and began to lay hands gently on the heads of each one of us. As they did so, they encouraged us to give God praise. I was a bit shy and did not know what to do, but I listened to others around me and some were singing, some were saying "Praise God", or "Jesus I love you", while others were saying "Hallelujah". I began to quietly say "Hallelujah" and one of the leaders said, "That's it, son, go on giving God praise".

Encouraged that I was doing it right, I became a little bolder and louder. In fact, everyone around me was getting louder so I continued with my "Hallelujahs" but then my tongue seemed to get stuck in my mouth and I could not get the words out. Pastor Morrison was on hand to encourage me saying, "Let it flow John, let it flow" and with that, flow it did. Like a torrent this strange language came up from my stomach and out of my mouth, it was incredible and so joyous.

I do not know how long this went on for, but I do know the meeting had been dismissed and I was still flowing with this new language. Eventually Sylvia and some friends led me out of the building and it was as though I was drunk; I could hardly stand, but I felt ecstatic. Sylvia did say she was a bit of a spectator while all this was going on and felt a bit left out. Happily, a few months later at another church, Sylvia too experienced this same phenomenon.

To say this experience changed me is a massive understatement. Even the next morning at the bus stop on my way to work I was aware something was different. Instead of talking about the weather, football or what was on television the night before, I was telling people what had happened to me at church. I told people at the office too; it was the most natural thing for me to do that; it just overflowed; I could not contain it.

Sylvia noticed I was different too. I was able to express myself more openly and, in some settings, I became more of an extrovert than an introvert. Something had definitely taken place inside me and as a person I was far more secure.

It's now over 48 years since that wonderful night and I am so glad I was able to receive that Baptism in the Holy Spirit with the gift of speaking in tongues. I have, metaphorically speaking, climbed many mountains and passed through many valleys since then, but it has been great to be able to do so in the power of the Holy Spirit.

If you have never received the Baptism in the Holy Spirit and the gift of tongues, then let me encourage you to open up your heart and earnestly desire it from your Heavenly Father. It is his promise for you, and it will make such a wonderful difference in your life as you journey on being filled afresh with the Holy Spirit every day.

* * *

35. ON MY KNEES

Sylvia was not one for writing lots of things in the margins of her Bible, but after one particular message that touched her, she wrote, "We are not nearly desperate enough". I guess that is true so often. How frequently we read in the Gospel stories of desperate people who received their miracles. There are many, but immediately I recall the paralysed man who was lowered through the roof to Jesus, the woman who pressed through the crowd to touch the hem of Jesus' garment and the blind man who shouted out all the more for Jesus to give him his sight.

There is a multitude of ways we can pray of course, including sitting down; eyes open or shut; prostrate on the floor; standing up; bowing down; marching around at home; in the park etc. We can pray silently, quietly or out loud and sometimes very loud. These days as there is much more to thank God for and many more people in my life in need of prayer, I find that sometimes I start off on my knees, then stand up for a while and progress to marching around.

Thinking back to what Sylvia had written in her Bible, I have to say that there have been times in my life when in desperation I have thrown myself to my knees and poured my heart out to God, often in tears. One such time was when we lived in an upstairs maisonette and our three daughters were all under the age of two. I would go off to work each day, leaving Sylvia with the children. If she needed to go out to the shops, or visit someone, it was quite an ordeal to get the twin pushchair and the girls down four flights of stairs. Then, of course, there was the physical aspect of carrying the shopping back home. I became very aware of how difficult life had become for Sylvia and how this was adversely affecting her and the children.

I desperately wanted to do something to make life easier for all concerned, but I had no idea what could be done. For several mornings before going off to the office, therefore, I would fall on my knees, bury my head in the armchair and cry out to God for help. It was during one of those mornings that an idea (almost an inner voice) came into my mind. "Sylvia needs to learn to drive," I thought.

I tried to put the idea out of my mind because it seemed too ridiculous for words, but day after day the thought persisted.

Eventually I plucked up the courage to suggest this to Sylvia, to which she responded with a derisory laugh. Seeing that I was serious, however, she began to ask how that would be possible since financially we were only just managing to pay our way week by week on my wage as a typist. I probably responded with something like "Well, if it's of God, He will make it happen".

A short while later we got to know a man "who just happened to be a driving instructor". He was also a Christian and because of our situation he offered to give Sylvia driving lessons at half the usual price. Thus it was, that Sylvia began to learn to drive and though there were a few hairy moments along the way, she did actually pass her driving test first time; what a joyous moment that was!

About the same time, a friend asked Sylvia, "What sort of car are you praying for?"

It never occurred to us at the time to be so specific, but in the end Sylvia, with a shrug of the shoulders said, "I trained in a Ford Escort, so I may as well have one of them".

Fast forward a few short weeks to one Saturday morning and there was a knock on our door. It turned out to be a couple called Chris and Janet, people I had met in Croydon about six months earlier when I spoke at a weekend youth event at their church. After inviting them in and getting over our initial shock, they joined us for breakfast.

Later in the morning as we were sitting chatting, Chris said, "You are probably wondering why we are here".

We said that we were, and they told us they were on their way to a holiday in the Peak District and just stopped off to see us. With that, Chris lobbed over a set of keys that landed in Sylvia's lap.

"What are these," she said somewhat incredulously.

"They are your car keys," said Chris.

"But I don't have a car," replied Sylvia.

"You do now", said Chris, "take a look outside".

Chris and Janet walked with us over to the window and pointed to a car. "It's that light blue Ford Escort, 18 months old with 11,000 miles on the clock".

They went on to explain that they had two cars and God had clearly told them to give one of them to us. Apparently, ever since my visit to their church they had prayed for us as a family every day.

We went outside to have a closer look and go for a short ride around the local area. It truly was amazing, and Chris and Janet did not even know that Sylvia had said, "In that case I will have a Ford Escort", but God had heard it.

Sylvia enjoyed that car so much and for several years it served us so well travelling around the country. It was a car which provided us with many happy family memories.

So are you desperate enough to throw yourself on your knees and cry out to God? You never know, he may just hear you!

* * *

36. SCHOOL REPORTS

The very title of this article fills me with a certain amount of dread. Overall, I did not enjoy my schooldays, apart from sports that is! I was always under the impression that I was useless when it came to learning, because when exam results came around, I was often in the bottom six out of a class of around 40 pupils. I should have comforted myself with the truth that this was at least the "A stream" – yes there was a "B stream" with an equal number of children.

Suffice to say that when I reached the age of 15, I could not wait to get out of school and into work.

School assemblies, do you remember those? I actually liked them, because at least it was out of the classroom. On the subject of assemblies, it was always a bit more exciting when we had a visitor come along to give the teachers a break. The animal man was always very popular with his array of reptiles and such like. I remember we had a magician come in from time to time and he was always very popular and then there were the people with disabilities, who were always interesting if only for the novelty value. Little did I think at the time that one day I would be fulfilling that role.

Yes, over the years I have had a lot of fun visiting schools and colleges, either to talk about the challenges of being blind, or my Christian faith, or even both.

One great memory was when I was at a school in Sutton Coldfield for a whole week speaking in Religious Education classes. I always found that being blind, the kids were very sympathetic towards me and they gave me their rapt attention. I was just commencing my presentation on the first lesson of the day one morning, when the head teacher entered the room, saying to me that he was sorry, but a surprise visitor had come along and would like to share the day with me. This surprise person was none other than Barry McGuire. That's probably not a name that would mean much to you, but in the 1960s Barry had a big hit record called *Eve of Destruction*. Prior to that he had two other hits with the band New Christy Minstrels called *Three Wheels on my Wagon* and *Green Green*. To say I was awe-struck is putting it mildly. I was fully prepared to sit back and let Barry take over and tell his story, but he said "No sir, this is your gig and I will do whatever you ask me to do".

I was, as they say today, blown away by his humility.

For the rest of the day we worked together as a great team and I am still in contact with Barry, who is now 84, to this day.

Children and teachers can sometimes be embarrassing. Let's take the children first. I had been talking with a group of 10/11 year old in their R.E. class, working hard to explain how Jesus does miracles today, though sometimes not in the way we expect. At the end of my talk the teacher asked the kids to put their hand up if they had a question for me. Several hands went up right away and the first boy to ask me a question, said rather cheekily, "As a blind man John, how do you get hold of women?"

Needless to say, I was quite taken aback and bluffed it off by saying something like, "I'll tell you afterwards".

Then there was the embarrassing teacher. I had done my bit in talking about how I went blind as a 19-year-old and then how it was, adjusting to my new life. The teacher came alongside me, saying she was a neighbour of mine and how well I got around quite independently. She then invited questions but was surprised that the first question was for her.

A young lady about 12 years of age asked, "Is it right Miss that you do not have a television and if so, why not".

The teacher boldly replied, "Well if we have a television, my husband and I would never have it off!".

The whole class erupted into laughter, as the embarrassed teacher, tried to rectify her mistake. As often happens in such circumstances, she only dug herself a deeper and deeper hole.

I was aware that my going into schools would often give the teacher a break from the normal routine and the ingenuity that some of them showed was to be admired. I remember going to Malvern Hall School in Solihull and I was invited by a teacher to speak at his English class. He told the kids that I was going to tell my story of how I became blind, how I came to terms with that tragedy and then how I came to believe in a loving God. He explained to them that they needed to pay attention, make notes if they wanted to, because their homework would be to write an essay on what they had heard.

As I said at the beginning I did not enjoy my own schooldays, but I have certainly appreciated the many times I have been able to go back to schools since and tell my story of living with disability and sharing my life with the God who has loved me with an everlasting love.

* * *

37. SEVEN UP!

A dentist once told me that if I insisted on having fizzy drinks then make it "7up" because that would not damage my teeth. I took that to heart and, even though my preferred choice would still be (and often is) Coca Cola, I do drink my fair share of 7up to keep my teeth and the dentist happy! 7up has been around in its present form since 1936 but was available under a different name from 1929. As interesting as that may or may not be to you, it is not the drink I wish to focus on, but seven "ups" I hope will spur you on in your walk with God.

1. Wake Up

The Bible has much to say about churches and individuals who fall asleep spiritually. In Isaiah, God had to say "Awake, awake oh Zion for the Glory of the Lord is now upon you…" In Ephesians we read "Wake up oh sleeper and rise from the dead" and in Revelation several of the churches have to be roused from their sleepy state and return to their first love.

It's always good to have a regular spiritual health check-up. It is so easy to think we are okay, when in actual fact we are being gently lulled off into a Christian slumberland of going through the motions. That's not good enough, friends. God himself said I want you red hot, otherwise I will vomit you out of my mouth. Wake up then, the alarm is sounding.

2. Sit Up

In Ephesians we read that we have been raised up to sit with Christ in Heavenly places. As believers, you and I have been lifted up to that place of authority where, as joint heirs with Jesus, we have authority to rule and reign over our circumstances as well as decreeing blessings over people and the world. Karen Carpenter sang, "I'm on top of the world looking down on creation… your [God's] love put me on top of the world".

3. Stand Up

The hymn-writer had it spot on, "Stand up, stand up for Jesus, you Soldiers of the Cross. Lift high His royal banner, it must not suffer loss. From victory to victory his army He will lead, till every foe is vanquished and Christ is Lord indeed." This is not the time to take a back seat or rest on your laurels but rise up in your calling and be all that God has called you to be.

4. Speak Up

In order to fulfil your call, you may have to speak up, no longer being the quiet one in the crowd, content to pray and let others do the talking. This is your time to move out of the shadows and into the full light of the midday sun. What God has put in your heart needs to be seen and heard. If you don't do it or say it, then who will?

5. Shut Up

The Bible has a lot to say about the power of the tongue and there is even a whole chapter devoted to it in James chapter 3. I am convinced the main reason why we do not see miracles in our own lives and the lives of others is down to the misuse of the tongue. In Colin Urquhart's book *Faith for the Future* the story was told of a family (maybe his own) who around the dinner table spoke so much negativity. They decided to retrain themselves to speak positively and he said, it took them many months. Words are very powerful and will either build up or tear down. Some people say, "If you can't say anything good then say nothing at all," and that's not a bad maxim to live by. Psalm 34 reminds us that if we want to live long on the earth then "keep your tongue from evil and your lips from telling lies".

6. Cheer Up

In John 16 Jesus says to his disciples "In the world you will have trouble but cheer up for I have overcome the world". There are enough miserable people in the world, without Christians getting in on the act too! Jesus was, I believe, great fun to be around. We read that He was anointed with the oil of gladness above all of his fellows. A friend of mine wrote a song called *You Can't Keep the Joy Down for Long* and one of the lines says "I've tried and I've tried to be miserable, but I can't keep the joy down for long". That's how it is when you are full of the Holy Spirit; He gives the oil of joy for mourning and the garment of praise for the spirit of heaviness. It's quite okay, therefore, to say to someone "Cheers" for in so doing you are bestowing a blessing of cheerfulness upon them.

7. Look Up

I remember at school one particular teacher, if he saw a child looking downcast, or lost in thought with their head down, he would walk over, put his index finger under their chin and say "Chin up". There is something about looking up that exudes an air of confidence and positivity. No matter what you are going through, if you are a

Christian, you can look up because you are on the victory side. Jesus is still Lord and in the final analysis Jesus said, "Lift up your head because your redemption draws near".

Thirsty work this – I think I will pop to the fridge and get a can of coke – oops sorry I mean 7up, of course!

* * *

38. SILVER LININGS

I guess we are all looking for silver linings anywhere we can at the moment. This week, the assisted-living accommodation in which I am pleased to dwell, adopted the strictest of measures by putting us in total lockdown. What that means for me and my fellow residents is that we are not allowed any visitors whatsoever and we are strongly discouraged from leaving our apartments, let alone the building.

Now for that silver lining. There is a word I have come to like and that is discombobulated, and I have unsuccessfully in the past, looked for ways I could use it in my writing. Hey presto! This is that time. A quick look at the dictionary definition reveals to us that this word, amongst many other things, means confused, upset, frustrated and disconcerted. Well I think that sums up how I feel at this time perfectly and I am sure it is how the great majority of us are feeling.

I have not felt so excited about a word since I heard dear old Henry Blowfeld on Test Match Special refer to the soporific pigeons. After "Blowers" used that expression a number of times, there was nothing else for it, I had to make a dash for my dictionary; pre-Google you see.

I love words, whether in the form of poetry, song lyrics, or even those used in emails or texts to remind someone how much you love and appreciate them.

One of my all-time favourite bands "The Bee Gees" wrote a big hit song called *Words* and in that song Robin Gibb, in that magnificent falsetto voice sings the refrain "It's only words and words are all I have to take your heart away".

Not surprisingly, God uses a similar approach in seeking to communicate his love to us. Back in the story of creation in Genesis, the first recorded thing that God said is "Let there be light" and there was. That's not a bad prayer for us to replicate now; that the world be filled with the light of God.

Thankfully, God does not just use wonderful words, but he backs them up with action. I love the verse in the Bible that says, "God warmly commended his love to us in that while we were still far away from Him, He came and died for us so that we could live. That's pretty stunning don't you think?

Discombobulated certainly, even soporific at times with so many things having closed down, but my faith is strong and rooted in the promises of God, hundreds of them in fact. Why not use this time of isolation to dig out some of the big questions of life and, in so doing, this for you could be life-transforming? You never know you could have an epiphany moment! My goodness that's another great word I have not used before. Two silver linings in one day; I think I had better go and lie down.

* * *

39. SING AND DANCE!

"Rejoice, rejoice, and again I say, rejoice!" These words were penned a long time ago not by someone who had just won the Lottery, but by Paul, who had been severely flogged and thrown into prison simply for doing the will of God. Paul, a highly intelligent and former devout Jew, had once terrorised the Christian Church, cursing and killing any who dared stand in his way.

After his dramatic conversion to Christ on the Damascus road, however, Paul underwent a radical transformation. God turned him around 180 degrees to the point whereby he became as passionate for Christ as he once was against him and maybe even more so. Now with the glorious sense of being forgiven and with the certainty of eternal life reverberating in his bones he fearlessly preached to all, "Believe in the Lord Jesus Christ and you will be saved".

It appears as if Paul received a mighty revelation right at the beginning of his new life as a Christian. He realised there had been a great change take place within his very being. Truths like "If anyone is in Christ he is a new creation – the old things have passed away and all things have become new", "It's Christ in you, the hope of glory" and "If the same Spirit that raised Christ from the dead lives in you, he will quicken (make alive) your mortal body" became his driving force. As you read of the way in which Paul bounced back from major setbacks and disappointments you are left with the feeling that inside him was an irrepressible, powerful Holy Spirit.

This was never more in evidence than in Acts 16, Paul in the same prison referred to above, with his friend Silas, was singing hymns and worshipping God at midnight even though he must have been cold, sore from the flogging and maybe even wondering why God had allowed this to happen. There was a prophetic song in Paul's heart; a burning fire that nothing could quench – those rivers of living water just had to flow out. The more you squeezed Paul the more the rivers of praise would flow.

The praises ascended into the very presence of God and moved his heart. An earthquake came, the prison doors flew open, the chains fell off every prisoner and the jailer and all his household were saved and baptised. Wow! The power of an anointed song and the sacrifice of praise.

No matter what you are going through right now, just maybe it is time to sing and rejoice in the presence of God. He is worthy of your praise no matter what your circumstances and you never know, your breakthrough could just be at hand. He is, after all, "Lord of the breakthrough".

Do not assume that because you are surrounded by trouble on every hand that you are outside the will of God. In fact, the opposite may be true if Paul is anything to go by.

In the book of Daniel we read the story of the three Hebrew young men who refused to bow down to the King's golden statue and as a result they were thrown into the furnace. The King was so enraged at their stance that he ordered the fire to be heated up seven times hotter than usual. The three young men were thrown, bound and gagged into the fire and later when the furnace door was opened by the guards just to check that they were well and truly dead, they were astonished to find four men in the fire dancing and free from their bonds – they were moved to exclaim that the fourth man was like the Son of God. What a revelation that must have been! Again, as we saw with Paul above, God used this time of testing as an opportunity to reach the lost. The evil King on discovering what had happened, fell to his knees and worshipped God.

Are you going through fiery trials right now? May I suggest that you begin to dance before the Lord. Remember King David, taking off his clothes and dancing before the Lord with all his might. When his wife ridiculed him, the King responded with these wonderful words, "I'll become even more undignified than this".

It's time for you and me to become far less dignified in our praise. We need to be extravagant with our praises, sing with a loud voice and dance exuberantly before the King of Kings and Lord of Lords. He is worthy and, you never know, our sweet worship may just thrill the heart of God so much that he is moved to act on our behalf and on behalf of others too in a remarkable way.

***

40. STAND UP AND LIVE – THE CHOICE IS YOURS

Have you ever been gripped by fear? In my autobiographical book

Fear, Fun and Faith I described the many fears that blighted my life up until the time I met Jesus at the age of 21. Jesus then, little by little, began to give me victory over each of those fears but, now and again, fear comes knocking at my door.

Back in the 1980s when my family and I had moved to live in Redruth, Cornwall so I could attend Bible College, I developed a serious problem with my left ear. Without going into the gory details, I had a foul-smelling discharge, which the Doctor said could be cancerous. I had a biopsy and was awaiting the results when one night, I awoke in the early hours shaking with fear. I had had a most vivid dream that I was attending my own funeral. I was so scared and I went downstairs, dropped to my knees and buried my head in the armchair sobbing. Part of that was because I was afraid of what the biopsy might show up and part of it was that I felt ashamed that as a Christian I was frightened of dying.

I don't know how long I was there in that state, but I was very broken up inside when suddenly deep within me came this phrase, "You can lie down and die, or you can stand up and live – the choice is yours". Immediately I shot to my feet and stood to attention and declared "I shall not die but I will live to declare your works, Oh Lord." (Psalm 118:17).

As I spoke out those words, strength and confidence filled my being and peace flooded my heart. I have spoken that Scripture hundreds of times since and those who know me, will confirm that I have declared the works of God up and down this land whenever I have been given the opportunity.

I have discovered the truth of what it says in Proverbs 18:21 "Life and death are in the power of the tongue…"

Thankfully, my biopsy results came back all clear and a simple operation was able to deal with the discharge. From time to time fear comes against us all and that may be the case for you now, especially in these very testing times. I've heard it said that when fear comes knocking at your door, send faith to answer it. If the parcel delivery person comes to your house and says, "I have a box of poisonous snakes, will you sign for them?" You have a choice. Of course you would be crazy to accept them. In the same way, do not accept fear, which comes from the Devil "The Lord has not given you a spirit of fear, but a spirit of power, love and a sound mind." (2 Timothy 1:7)

Similarly, someone has said, you cannot stop birds flying overhead, but you can stop them nesting in your hair. In other words do not allow fearful, negative thoughts to take root in your mind. Instead, do just as Jesus did when the Devil came against him while he was fasting for 40 days and nights, speak what the Bible says about you. It's worth getting to know the Bible, especially while you are shut in for who knows how many weeks, because there are hundreds of amazing promises in there from God just for you.

Here is just one, "For I know the plans I have for you says the Lord, plans to do you good and not to do you harm, to give you a future and a hope." (Jeremiah 29:11) That is God's heart for you, because He is good, and He passionately loves you.

So what are you going to do? You can lie down and die, or you can stand up and live – the choice is yours. Can you join me in boldly declaring "I shall not die, but I shall live to declare your works, Oh Lord"?

* * *

41. TAKE YOUR HARP DOWN FROM THE WILLOW TREE

Rivers of Babylon by Boney M topped the UK singles chart for four weeks in 1978 and became the biggest selling record of that year. The lyrics are taken almost exclusively from Psalm 137, with one verse also from Psalm 19. Interestingly, this set me off thinking if any other popular songs had been taken direct from the Bible and I can only think of one. *Turn, turn, turn*, the song composed by Pete Seeger, the American folk singer, was a hit for The Byrds and the lyrics from this song are taken from Ecclesiastes 3. If you can recall any other song taken from Scripture like this, perhaps you would enlighten me.

Psalm 137 is, I believe, very relevant for where we are today in terms of this coronavirus pandemic. The people of God had been brutalized by the army of King Nebuchadnezzar. They had seen many men, women and children barbarically killed, before they themselves were dragged off into exile. God's people were utterly demoralized, grieving and longing for their freedom; they just wanted to be back home. I am sure many of us can relate to those feelings and emotions.

Things were made a whole lot worse when the Israelites were taunted by their enemy. "Sing us the songs of Zion" they were told, but they did not feel like singing. They were sad and licking their wounds, they had even hung up their harps on the willow trees.

This reminds me of being at a professional football game in the UK. When one team is winning, the opposing supporters taunt their opposing fans with chants like, "You're not singing any more" or "You only sing when you're winning". Cruel isn't it and it's designed to humiliate and demoralize the opposition.

A lot of what is going on today is being used by our Enemy to bring discouragement, despondency, and grief into our lives. If we have lost our joy, he is probably yelling over us "You're not singing any more" or "You only praise God when things are good and going well".

God's people said, "How can we sing the Lord's song in a strange land?" We hear the word "unprecedented" a lot at the moment and these certainly are strange days in which we are living. The song of the Lord is powerful and it's mighty to sing even in a strange land or situation. The Devil is always wanting to steal our joy and our peace. If you are experiencing that right now, then perhaps it's time to take your harp down from the willow tree and begin making music to the Lord your God. As we read in Isaiah 61 "He will give us beauty for ashes, the oil of joy for mourning and the garment of praise for the spirit of heaviness". It won't happen automatically, it is up to each one of us to physically make a move towards that willow tree and take down our harp. Then start to play, start singing and start dancing before the Lord. Before you know where you are, you will experience again the joy of the Lord, which is your strength and the peace of God which passes all human understanding.

In so doing the circumstances around us may not have changed but we have and, once again, we have a rejoicing heart.

Now let me pick up my harp and dig out my Boney M single!

* * *

42. TASTE AND SEE!

When you are without sight you are dependent, to a large degree, on what other people tell you. There are many occasions when I allow people to make up my mind for me and of course that is not necessarily a good thing, especially from an independence viewpoint. One of those areas for me was food. For instance, people close to me would sometimes say, "You wouldn't like that" and I would just accept it.

One day I was staying with some people in the South West of England. At breakfast, my host said to me, "John, I am terribly sorry, but I have run out of cereals, but I do have some grapefruit. "That's okay," I said, "I am not much of a breakfast person." "But I feel really bad about this" replied the lady, "won't you please have some grapefruit?" "No honestly, I don't like grapefruit" I responded firmly.

Sitting next to me at the table was my blind friend Peter Jackson, a full time Gospel pianist and preacher. Peter, never short of a word or three, entered into the conversation by saying to our concerned host, "Knowing John, he's probably never tried grapefruit." "That's right, I haven't" came my instant reply. "Well in that case, how do you know you won't like it then?" said Peter, while chuckling at the same time. I knew I was beginning to lose this little debate as I responded feebly, "Because other people have told me I won't like it".

Now Peter, ever the opportunist to make a spiritual point, came back with, "You are just like the people who say they have no time for Christianity when they have never given Jesus a chance with their lives, it is nonsensical. Give the grapefruit a try for yourself and then if you don't like it okay, but really it is very refreshing." "Will you have some then, John?" said our kind host who had been an amused bystander to this light-hearted discussion. "Yes, okay then, but just a little" I said, with Peter choking back the giggles at my side.

Well, as you will probably realise by now, although the grapefruit tingled initially on my tongue, I have to confess that it was not anywhere near as sour as I had been led to believe, in fact it was rather nice and as Peter had rightly said, very refreshing. Now I love grapefruit, but to think of all those years I missed out just because I was allowing myself to be controlled by other people's ideas and opinions instead of looking into it for myself so that I could make an informed judgement.

Oh yes, and Peter was correct in his comment that many people do make the same mistake when it comes to the big questions in life. We often mimic other people's opinions or experiences instead of doing some research and finding out for ourselves. I still think one of the most important questions is, "Where will I go when I die?" or "Is there such a place as Heaven or Hell and if so how do I get to one and avoid the other?" I have always felt that these are important questions to be asking and that, unlike the grapefruit, which is far more trivial (sorry grapefruit worshippers) the matter of life, death and eternity are far too important for me to rely on someone else's opinions. I have to know for myself.

I have discovered a little verse in Psalm 34 of the Bible that says "Oh taste and see that the Lord is good" which, thankfully, I now have and I've discovered He is even better than grapefruit; in fact he made the grapefruit so how cool is that then?

The above is an extract from the Fun section of my book, "Fear Fun and Faith".

* * *

43. THE BIRDS ARE SINGING!

Singing is a lot of fun. It brings refreshment to the one who is singing and spreads joy all around, like a smile. Doctors now tell us, what I learned from the Bible long ago, that it is a healthy thing to have a song resonating from the heart. In my childhood I can recall that people such as the milkman or the bus driver would often be singing or whistling as they worked and, as they did so, it spread an aura of joy. People don't seem to do that kind of thing much today so let's start a campaign to get people singing again.

Have you noticed that if people do speak in the morning, which can be rare I must admit, then they might say "Morning". It has led me to ask, "Where has the good gone in good morning?" I now make a point of saying "Good morning", even when it is pouring with rain. One person said to me "What is good about it?" and I replied, "Well you are alive aren't you? You could be dead". I think it brought them up with a jolt.

In times of hardship singing has been a great antidote to worry, it has united the people and inspired so called ordinary people to perform great feats of courage. In World War 1 one of the great hit songs was *Pack Up Your Troubles in Your Old Kit Bag and Smile, Smile, Smile*. It is a very hard thing to sing for much more than 10 minutes and stay in depression. Something happens on the inside of us as we sing a joyful song that somehow dispels the darkness around and we begin to see things from a different perspective.

Again, I have had to learn this secret for myself and the revelation has come through reading the Bible and discovering that God is a God of song, dance, exuberant joy, and a great deal of fun. I discovered that God loves me so much that he sings over me and dances around me with great excitement. He loves music because he invented music.

God also had fun in creation, especially when naming the animals. Of all of his creation I just love the birds of the air, apart from the pigeons when they drop stuff on my head in Birmingham City Centre that is! It is a wonderful thing to wake up in the morning to the sound of the birds singing their cheerful song of joy. They just don't seem to get depressed. Many of us we wake up blurry-eyed saying, rather grumpily, "Good Lord, it's morning" instead of awaking bright-eyed and bushy-tailed with a cheery, "Good morning, Lord, thank you for a brand new day".

Not so with the birds however, they appear to be bright and cheery everyday no matter what the weather.

Budgerigars have been pets in our family since I was a child. When I was at home with Mum and Dad, nearly all budgies seemed to be called Joey and ours was no exception. Since being married we have only had three budgies. The first was yellow looking rather like a canary. We called him "Chico" and he was quite a little character. He bounced up and down to the Tamla Motown song, *Tears of a Clown* by the Miracles and he used to love coming out of his cage and flying around the room. He would walk on the floor (a dangerous thing to do with a blind man around) and then take off and land on anything he could find from chairs to vases. He also loved landing on the heads of people much to Sylvia's terror. It got to the stage where Sylvia could not stand being in the room while Chico was flying around. As I had developed a practice of getting up at 6am to get ready for work, pray, read the Bible etc, it was an ideal opportunity to open Chico's cage and let him have his fly around before the rest of the family got up.

I remember one Saturday morning I was sitting in the armchair, concentrating very hard on reading part of my Braille Bible and Chico flew on to my lap and he walked across the page I was reading. I found this quite cute and amusing, until Sylvia walked in and said, "Do you know that the bird is pecking your Braille dots off the page?" At this I hastily flicked Chico off as I wondered to myself how many months had he been doing that? Was this the reason why I was finding so many Bible passages hard to read? Braille was difficult enough for me to read without Chico making it even more so. Pecking dots off, here and there, can change a word into something completely different. Nowadays if I go out to give a Bible talk, I will sometimes preface the message by saying "If this is heresy, don't blame me but blame the budgie!".

Later we had two budgies – they actually belonged to our son Ian, but because of his job they spent most of their time with us, being fed and watered by Sylvia. The birds (one blue and one green) were named by Ian as Diamond and Denver, by way of a tribute to his two favourite singers Neil Diamond and John Denver. To help us, and particularly our grandchildren, know which one was which I made up the following rhyme:

Blue Diamond and Denver Green,
The most beautiful budgies you've ever seen.
They whistle and play throughout the day,
Blue Diamond and Denver Green.

Diamond outlived Denver and he too was an inspiration. Despite living his life entirely in a cage (even when the door was open, he would not fly out) nevertheless he was so cheerful. He did not like being alone. He loved company, particularly the sound of women's voices and lively music. He whistled away for hours on end and when I arrived home from work, he always gave me a most chirpy welcome as if he was really glad to see me. Yes, there's no doubt about it in my view, birds are a lot of fun and we can all learn a lesson from their cheerful songs.

Some parts of this article are taken from the Fun section of my book "Fear Fun and Faith".

* * *

44. THE CREDIBILITY GAP

At one particular time of my life, it was my privilege to count as friends three men who were all Trading Standards Officers in different areas of the country. Just one part of their varied job description was to bring to account individuals or companies whose products did not "Do what it said on the tin". In other words, there was a credibility gap. They said one thing, but did another. In more serious cases, individuals were stopped from trading and companies closed down.

I have often wondered how I as an individual, or indeed hundreds of local churches across the UK, would fare if we were put under the scrutiny of Trading Standards.

Reading in Luke 7, I see that Jesus attended a funeral and raised a young man from the dead. He was moved with compassion and then gave the boy back to his mother. A short while after that, Jesus receives a message from his cousin John the Baptist, who is in prison. John's friends ask Jesus, "Are you the Messiah sent from God, or should we look for another?" Jesus replied by saying, "The blind see, the deaf hear, the lame walk, the dead are raised and the Gospel of the Kingdom is being preached. Happy are those who are not offended in me".

Focusing on what Jesus did and said, what a spectacular demonstration of God's love and power!

In the opening verses of Luke 9 we read that Jesus called his friends together and he gave them power and authority to drive out demons and cure all diseases. He then sent them out, two by two, and they marveled at what they were able to do in Jesus' name.

There are some Christian traditions which say that experience was just for the Church Age and, once the last of the Apostles had died, then it was all over. Others say that once the Bible was put into print, we had God's full revelation and there is no need for miracles or signs and wonders now. I must admit that, believing that message, puts very little pressure on us to believe God and stretch our faith for much.

Thank God, I belong to the stream of the Church that interprets Scripture as if it is God's living word for today and that we are able to do, in His Name, all that he said we could do. Jesus said to his disciples, when they were astonished that even the demons obeyed him, "Greater things you will do than these".

On almost every page of the Gospels and Acts of the Apostles we read about mighty miracles taking place. I have been a Christian for over 50 years now and, in that time, I have seen some exciting things. I have been present on a few occasions when people have been wonderfully healed and I have even been used myself on occasions to bring healing to people.

I cannot help but wonder, though, if a Trading Standards Officer examined my life and compared it to the pages of the New Testament, would I fall far short of "What it said on the tin"? Then how about if the Trading Standards Office instructed their team to read the Gospels and Acts of the Apostles and then sent them into every UK church for one month, how many would be closed down?

I would say, the greatest miracle is someone coming to know Jesus, receiving forgiveness for their sins and having their lives totally transformed by the power of the Holy Spirit. Some local churches see that happen on a regular basis but, sadly, my guess is that hundreds across the country may not see that happen from one year to the next. They may be loving, caring fellowships of God's people, but is that all they were really called to be and do?

The pages of the New Testament are exciting and dynamic because people encountered Jesus and his ability to bring transformation of spirit, soul and body. Now Jesus, as I understand it has delegated that authority to people like you and me.

As great as the UK church has been during this pandemic in terms of food banks, social care and such like, the cry of my heart is, "Where is the supernatural in terms of, healings, miracles and signs and wonders?" According to Romans 10:17, faith comes by hearing the preached word of God. So I pray that we will hear much more of this teaching from our pulpits so as to equip people like us to go out and do the work of the ministry, i.e. preach the gospel of the Kingdom, drive out demons, heal the sick so as to close that credibility gap.

* * *

45. THE GREATEST DISCOVERY

These are still early days in the coronavirus pandemic, especially for those of us who have been instructed to self-isolate for 12 weeks. It's also very early days for those like me, trying to manage without their football fix. No football; no cricket; no tennis; no F1; no golf; no rugby; just how is this sports-mad nation and world going to cope! Furthermore, no theatre trips, no music concerts, and no sunshine holidays.

Everything it seems, has been, or is being stripped away.

I always remember my Dad saying, "As a nation we will rue the day we stopped teaching our children the 10 Commandments. Number one commandment of course is "You shall have no other gods before me".

Every single one of us was created with the need to worship and if that worship does not go to the Lord God Almighty then it gets transferred to other people or things, but in the end, none of them truly satisfy.

I wonder, could God in his mercy, be allowing this virus for a season to cause us all to reevaluate the way we are building our lives. If we take time to think about the bigger issues then, what may look now like a disaster, could turn out to be the best thing to happen to our planet in many a long year. I am sure already, for instance, the environment is benefitting in so many ways.

You may not be able to quote the 10 Commandments, but Jesus came along and reduced them to just two. "Love the Lord your God with all your heart, all your soul, all your mind and with all your strength and then love your neighbour as you love yourself".

In the grand scheme of things, I wonder, could that be what the Great Architect is wanting to produce out of this time of severe testing?

If this enforced period of self-isolation enables you and your loved ones, to discover God as your loving Heavenly Father, Jesus Christ as your personal Saviour and the sweet Holy Spirit as your constant guide and friend, then you will have made the greatest discovery known to mankind.

***

46. TRIBUTES COME POURING IN

I am aware that there are a lot of sad stories around at the moment, mainly relating to deaths as a result of the coronavirus pandemic. Along with everyone else, I empathise and pray for those who have lost loved ones at this time, especially as a direct result of this evil virus.

Yesterday on the news, we heard the oft-repeated phrase "Tributes have been pouring in". This related in particular to the deaths of three well-known people. Tim Brooke-Taylor, remembered for many things but in particular, *I'm Sorry I'll Read That Again*, *The Goodies* and *I'm Sorry I Haven't a Clue*, and who succumbed to coronavirus. Sir Stirling Moss, one of the greatest racing drivers of all time, died at the age of 90 and then we heard that Peter Bonetti, the legendary Chelsea and England goalkeeper, had died at the age of 78. As I said, the tributes came flooding in as a mark of respect for the roles that these three men played in our national life.

There were also many other deaths from coronavirus in this country, but sadly for the great majority of these people, the tributes will not keep pouring in. Most will be remembered with dignity by their own small circle of family and friends, many unsung heroes among them.

On the flipside of course, whilst there are a great many deaths every day, there are also many thousands of births across the globe. Hopefully, the great majority of these new babies will bring joy and hope to their families and friends.

There is nothing like the birth of a new baby to lift the spirit. In the classic Johnny Mathis song, often played at Christmas, *When a Child is Born*, we have the opening verse:

A ray of hope flickers in the sky.
A tiny star lights up way up high.
All across the land, dawns a brand new morn.
This comes to pass when a child is born.

No tributes pouring in for a newborn baby, but lots of hope for its future.

One baby was born, however, who was different to any other birth in history and this was the person we have been celebrating this last Easter weekend. Jesus' birth was every bit as miraculous as his glorious resurrection.

Firstly, Jesus' virgin birth, along with the birthplace, had been prophesied on a number of occasions many years before. That in itself is remarkable, but immediately surrounding his birth there was a glorious visitation when a host of Heavenly Angels visited some working-class shepherds on their night shift. After the shepherds had overcome their great fear, the Angels brought a message to them about the birth of this baby in Bethlehem that would be good news to the whole earth, because this baby would bring peace, joy and goodwill to people everywhere.

The shepherds were so excited by what they heard, they did

something very irresponsible; they left their sheep and went in search of this baby. When they found him lying in a manger they bowed down and worshipped him.

Since then the tributes have come pouring in for this Jesus, who has shown himself to be the Prince of Peace and the Saviour of the World. That is certainly the case for millions of people, like me, who have come to know Jesus personally and appreciate the great many wonderful things He has done in our lives.

In the midst of the coronavirus pandemic, with all the fear that accompanies it, I pray you may come to know the Jesus, who came as a vulnerable baby and then died and rose again as a true man, thereby demonstrating his amazing love for us to give us victory over sin and death.

***

47. WANTED DEAD OR ALIVE

Like many children of my generation, I grew up loving the old western films and series. On the big screen actors such as John Wayne, Burt Lancaster, James Stewart and many more were making their names as would-be cowboys. Throughout the late 1950s, 60s and 70s western series were being shown on television virtually every night, just as the soaps are today. If my mates were out playing football, they would know not to call for me while *Wagon Train*, *Bonanza*, *Cheyenne* or any other of a host of westerns, was being shown.

Typical in those shows, was the scenario when someone had killed someone else, or even robbed a bank. The local sheriff would then issue a warrant for the arrest of the culprit or gang responsible. A poster would be displayed all over the locality, with a photograph of the suspect(s), together with the caption "Wanted Dead or Alive".

Many people who become Christians, wonder why they have so

much trouble. We should not be surprised at this, however, because Jesus said, "In the world you will have tribulation...". The Bible also says, "Many are the afflictions of the righteous". We could look at lots more Scriptures too, demonstrating that life as a Christian is going to be anything but "a stroll in the park". God has promised us joy though, which is our strength and that he will never leave us nor forsake us.

Having said that, let me come quickly to the point. The day you made a decision to follow Jesus Christ as your Lord and Saviour, a warrant went out for your arrest and it reads, "Wanted Dead or Alive".

In John 10:10 Jesus gives us a good news - bad news story. He gives us the bad news first. "The thief (Satan) has come to steal, kill and destroy". That's right, Satan wants to steal your faith in order to drag you off to the lake of fire with him and if he cannot do that then he will kill and destroy you, shunting you off to Heaven prematurely. Bad and scary news, eh? Well, it would be if Jesus had left it there, but He came up with the good news, "I have come to give you life and life in all of its abundant, overflowing goodness". My strong advice, therefore, is to stay close to Jesus and enjoy life to the full and with Him and to overcome every challenge as they come your way.

Once you have decided to follow Jesus then you will soon discover you are in a battle. The thrill is, though, that Jesus has already won the victory. On the Cross, He gave out a triumphant shout "It is finished". The battle had been won over Satan and now, those of us who are born again and adopted into God's family, are on the victory side. We are more than conquerors and our role is to serve Jesus and crush the Devil under our feet.

According to Luke 10:19 Jesus has given you and me power and authority to tread on serpents and scorpions (demons) and over all the power of the enemy and "nothing shall by any means hurt us". In the old western parlance, Jesus is the sheriff and we believers are the posse, hunting down the Devil. "For this purpose was the Son of God manifest, to destroy the works of the Devil" (1 John 3:8).

Following his resurrection, Jesus said "Simon, Simon, Satan has desired to have you and sift you like wheat, but I have prayed for you that your faith will not fail and when you have overcome go back and strengthen (encourage) your brothers" (Luke 22:31)

You will see from this that the Devil wants to steal your faith and that is why he seeks to discourage you and turn you away from God. It's encouraging to read that Jesus prays for us that our faith will not fail. He then says that once we have overcome, we can go out and encourage others.

One of my all-time favourite verses in the Bible is Acts 10:38 "God anointed Jesus of Nazareth with the Holy Spirit and power and He went about doing good and healing all who were oppressed by the Devil".

I love the way it says Jesus of Nazareth, rather than Son of God, or some other Heavenly title. This refers to Jesus the Son of man as he is sometimes called. Instead of Jesus of Nazareth, let me encourage you to put your name in there and then read it back to yourself many times. Let me try it for size. God anointed John Flanner with the Holy Spirit and power and he went about doing good and healing all who were oppressed by the Devil. That's my mission and that's my life calling. It is my reason to be here on planet Earth and yours too.

Make no mistake about it, you and I are wanted dead or alive by the powers of darkness, but fear not, we can go out full of the Holy Spirit, covered and protected by the blood of Jesus, doing acts of kindness all over the place and bringing the healing love of God to all who are being oppressed by the Devil.

Jesus is Lord and the Devil's a fraud!

***

48. WAS BLIND BUT NOW I SEE!

It's hard to think of a greater joy in life than being in front of an eager audience to explain what Jesus Christ means to me and how he has radically impacted my life. It really is quite exhilarating being able to share this good news with people. I have had the privilege over many years now to tell my story in a whole variety of settings, but in terms of adrenalin, nothing quite compares with going into a prison to do that!

My first experience of that was probably the scariest of all. I was invited, one Sunday morning to Winson Green Prison, to share my testimony with the inmates as part of their Sunday service. I cannot describe how nervous I was, and it was made no better when the prison chaplain appealed for quiet as we were about to begin the service. The Chapel itself felt cold and unfriendly, probably stone-built. There was the clanking of chains and handcuffs as the men piled in and the noisy chatter was incessant. The Chaplain's appeals for quiet seemed to fall on deaf ears for a while but, at least when we sang the first hymn, there was an effort on the part of some of the men to try to sing along in tune.

I was thinking to myself, "They do not listen very well to the Chaplain, so what hope is there for me?"

When my time came, the Chaplain gave a brief introduction, explaining that I was blind, then he called me up. I stepped forward nervously but did not realise there was a slight step of just two or three inches, which I managed to trip over and went stumbling forward. As I struggled to regain my composure and stand to my feet, I thought, "That's given them all a good laugh".

The thing was, there was total silence and from that moment you could have heard a pin drop. It was amazing that even in that harsh environment, I felt compassion spread across the room. I spoke for about 20 minutes and then the Chaplain indicated that there was time for one or two questions. I will never forget the first question. The man said how much he had enjoyed my talk, but then asked, "If you could give up your faith and receive your eyesight, would you do it?"

I boldly proclaimed, "No way, my faith in Jesus is everything to me".

Immediately the whole Chapel burst out with applause!

Many years later, my answer is still the same. John Newton, the former slave-trader, turned Christian, social reformer and prolific hymn-writer penned the classic line in *Amazing Grace*, "I once was blind, but now I see".

Of course, John Newton was never physically blind, but he was spiritually blind, until God opened the eyes of his understanding and he turned away from sin and embraced Jesus.

Christopher Duffley was born premature and blind, the child of drug addict parents. He was so small and disabled when he was born, he was not expected to live. Look him up, sometime, on YouTube and hear him singing *Open the Eyes of my Heart, Lord*... and see what God has done for him.

I promise you, after more than 50 years, having your eyes opened to the love of God as revealed through Jesus, is the most wonderful thing. To know Jesus as my Saviour, my Healer, my Deliver and my coming King is truly awesome. I discovered that Jesus said, "No longer do I call you servants, but friends" and true enough Jesus is my very best friend with whom I hang around every day.

By the way ... in January this year I received an email from a trusted friend in Australia who said that, while he was praying, I came to mind and he had a very strong sense that I am going to receive my sight. That encouraged and excited me so much. I wrote back and told him I would see him in Australia when I come out to tell my miraculous story. God can do it, there is nothing too hard for him and that's true for your life too.

49. WAY BACK INTO LOVE

On my wife's dementia journey, we passed through many stages. One of them involved television. Sylvia's two favourite programmes were, at one time, *Downton Abbey* and *Call the Midwife*. Once dementia had set in, however, these were no longer of interest to her. Very quickly she realized that she could not follow each new storyline and so she became disinterested.

One day she asked if she could watch *The Sound of Music* and she loved that because she could follow it, knew what was coming next, and it did not place a strain on her mind. *Pretty Woman* quickly followed as did *Robin Hood Prince of Thieves*, along with a few other well-known favourites. Truthfully, we watched these same half a dozen movies over and over and over again, but they gave Sylvia great pleasure.

Incredibly, we did manage to sneak one new movie into the general rhythm and happily she came to love it and watch it every bit as much as the others. This was *Music and Lyrics* starring Hugh Grant and Drew Barrymore. It is a simple romantic tale of an ailing pop singer, played by Hugh Grant, who lives in the past, bemoaning his current lack of chart success. An up and coming star, says she is a fan of the fading star and she invites him to write a hit song for her. Unfortunately, he is a musician and does not write lyrics, but he comes across a woman who does and together they write a belting new song that the public absolutely love.

Sylvia and I thought that this was a very touching and, in its own way, a powerful story. Two songs particularly caught our attention.

Don't Write Me Off is sung by Hugh Grant and the words offer hope to us all who have failed in some way or feel we have missed the boat in life. I would imagine many of us have felt at times as though we have made one mistake too many and now there is no hope. Don't write me off is a cry from the heart to say "I am not finished yet, this is not the end of the story" and sure enough, in the movie Hugh Grant's character is able to make the big comeback.

The same can be true for you and, even if the stuffing has been knocked out of you, if you simply turn to God, surrender to Jesus, He will dust you off, embrace you and put you back on the road again with a new found resilience. He knew what it was like to be cruelly nailed to a cross, die and be shut in a tomb, but that was not the end, He bounced back and lives on today in the lives of all who love Him. He, it is, who made you and He will never write you off because He believes in you and the destiny which is on your life.

The other song, which becomes the big smash hit, is called *Way Back into Love*. This is about a broken relationship and the heartache that brings. Lonely and with an aching heart the cry is for a way back into love. There are millions around the world who can relate to that and maybe you are one of them. Here again the good news lies in Jesus. He, it is, who offers you not only a way back into love, but an opportunity to be part of the greatest love story in the universe.

An old Sunday School song says, *Jesus' love is very wonderful* and believe me, it is. Two years after going blind at the age of 19, I was introduced to this message of Jesus' love for me. I accepted it by faith and surrendered my life to Him. Over 50 years on and not even the loss of my beloved wife, who I will see again one day, has been able to rob me of that amazing love that Jesus Christ and I share together. I promise you, there is a way back into love and it is through Jesus Christ and from that relationship everything else will flow.

Now go and watch the movie and discover that true romance is not dead after all! Then, just as happens at the end of the film, let God scoop you up in his arms and give you all the love you have ever craved.

* * *

50. WEAPONS OF MASS DESTRUCTION

It's interesting how words and phrases become synonymous with certain time periods. No doubt coronavirus, something we had never heard of until very recently, will always be associated with 2020, then across Europe, the word Brexit was coined and almost drove us crazy for the last few years.

Going back just a little further, the phrase "Weapons of Mass Destruction" tarnished much of Tony Blair's tenure as Prime Minister. We heard the phrase repeatedly on news broadcasts across the world, almost on a par with Brexit and coronavirus.

While reading the Bible a year or two back, I came across this verse in 2 Corinthians 10:4 "Our weapons are not carnal, but are mighty in God to the pulling down of strongholds". Straightaway it hit me, we have weapons of mass destruction in the spiritual realm. These weapons have been given to us by God to destroy the works of the Evil One. "For this purpose was the Son of God manifested, to destroy the works of the evil one." (1 John 3:8)

I truly believe that most of us, who call ourselves Christians, have very little idea of the power we have at our disposal and what we are supposed to do with it.

In Acts 1:8 Jesus said, "You will receive power (dynamite) when the Holy Spirit comes upon you and you will be my witnesses…."

So we have dynamite within us, if we have received the Holy Spirit's power. My question is, have you received that power for yourself? If not, desire the fullness of the Holy Spirit with all your heart so that you can begin to wield those weapons of mass destruction on your enemy, the Devil.

This is a massive subject and one in which I believe the UK Church needs to become more educated and trained up in. For now, though, let me just concentrate on a few aspects which are real to me.

PRAISE

Praise is an amazing weapon of mass destruction that God has given to us. There are many references in Scripture to this, but Psalm 8 tells us that out of the mouths of babes and infants he has ordained praise to still the voice of the avenger. This simply means that our praises, from the youngest to the oldest will shut the Devil up. The Bible says that he goes around like a roaring lion, but actually he has no teeth and his mouth needs to be shut. Your praises will do that.

THANKSGIVING

In Psalm 100 we read that we are to enter His gates with thanksgiving in our hearts and then, in 1 Thessalonians 5, it says "In everything give thanks for this is the will of God in Christ concerning you." A thankful heart lifts the atmosphere, disperses the gloom and creates and atmosphere of faith, hope and love.

PRAYER OF AGREEMENT

Matthew 18 tells that "if two of you on earth agree about anything they ask for, it will be done for them by my Father in Heaven." In the Old Testament we read that one will put a thousand to flight but two will put ten thousand to flight. I cannot do the maths beyond that, but it's extremely powerful when it comes to overcoming the Evil One. Agreement and unity is a very powerful weapon of mass destruction.

PRAYING IN TONGUES

This is another powerful weapon, whether undertaken as an individual or in a group. The Devil hates it when we speak in tongues, because he has not got a clue what we are saying. Our spirit is in direct communication with the Holy Spirit and, by faith, we believe we are praying those things which are in God's heart and according to His will.

FINAL THOUGHTS

This is by no means a comprehensive list of our weapons of mass destruction given to us by our God. This is just my small attempt to alert my friends to the spiritual reality that there is so much more to prayer than we have yet realised.

God has blessed his people with every spiritual blessing so that we can be trained up as mighty warriors, who are skilled in using their weapons of mass destruction. In so doing, we crush Satan under our feet and usher in the Kingdom of Heaven, preparing the way for the return of Jesus Christ as the Champion of the World.

* * *

51. WHAT'S YOUR HALLELUJAH LIKE?

Leonard Cohen's famous song *Hallelujah* was written as a lament, and the original poem contained many more verses than ended up in the eventual recordings by Jeff Buckley (my favourite version) and Alexandra Burke. Apparently, Leonard (if I can be so familiar) did not have the best of luck when it came to affairs of the heart and that, amongst others things, led to him suffering from depression - hence the song.

Incidentally, this song is the only one which has ever been number one and number two in the UK singles chart at the same time, recorded by the aforementioned artists.

One of the lines in the song, which really touches me and, which occurs several times, is "It's a cold and a broken Hallelujah". This reminds me of a beautiful verse in Isaiah 42:3 "A bruised reed he will not break and a smouldering wick he will not put out".

There are times in life when pressures come and weigh heavily upon us and we are only able to manage a cold and broken Hallelujah.

Maybe it has to come through gritted teeth, but let it come. If you feel like a bruised reed, or a smouldering wick, where the fire has almost been distinguished, let me encourage you to let out a Hallelujah to the Lord. It may be cold, it may be broken right now, but your God will receive it and return it with manifold blessings. Remember there is awesome power in the sacrifice of praise.

There is an amazing song that is doing the rounds and extremely popular in churches right now. *Raise a Hallelujah* is a battle song. It was given to someone prophetically one night/early morning as the church were praying for the young son of a church member, who was dangerously close to death. As the person concerned turned to God, these words flowed into him and soon the song was born. The boy was healed and raised to perfect health.

Take a look on YouTube, at *Raise A Hallelujah* by Jonathan and Melissa, Bethel Church. Listen to the short testimony and the song lyrics. Listen again ... and raise the loudest Hallelujah you can muster!

* * *

52. WHEN JOHNNY CASH SANG

I wonder if any singer has ever had such an impact on someone's life as Johnny Cash has had on mine? Before going on to explain, let me invite you to listen on YouTube to Garth Hewitt, one of my favourite Christian artists, singing *When Johnny Cash Sang 'Man in Black'*.

As Garth reminds us, "He took the side of forgotten ones". Johnny Cash often spoke up for the people who had no voice in this world and his songs touched my heart, particularly way back in the 1970s.

The first song to do this was actually a monologue called *Dear Mrs* and it is all about the prisoner waiting in his cell for the post to arrive. Day after day he watched in vain, with tears in his eyes, as the guard delivering the mail passed by his cell. That spoke to me very clearly, as someone who enjoyed writing and receiving letters, I thought that this is something I could do.

On enquiring how to go about it I discovered that, first of all, I had to undergo a six week training course which involved me going to the office of a Probation Officer in Birmingham and learning all the do's and don'ts about communicating with prisoners. It seemed like a long-winded process to go through just to write a letter, but I got there in the end and for several years I communicated with a few prisoners, hopefully bringing them some comfort.

Then there was the story I mentioned in a recent posting where Sylvia had been reading to me a book called *The New Johnny Cash*. I had been so thrilled with this book that I wanted everyone to read it. It was a heart-warming story of one man's redemption and the power of love. This led to me writing to one of the presenters at Radio Birmingham (now WM) and that, in turn, led to me not only talking enthusiastically about the book on air, but ultimately to me reviewing new Christian record releases on the radio for nearly 15 years.

Finally, Johnny Cash impacted me hugely when a film, *The Gospel Road*, which he had financed himself, was released. The musical was filmed in Israel and told of the birth, life, death and resurrection of Jesus, all narrated by Johnny Cash and with scriptures taken directly from the Bible.

I was so excited about this movie that I decided to hire the film for one month. In those days, of course, it was all on open-reel tapes. I also employed a local Christian film company to travel around with me to show the film. Within that month we went to schools, colleges, churches and country and western clubs. It was an amazing month and I was thrilled that the good news of Jesus was going to so many people.

At one club, The Silver Saddle, in Erdington, a man dressed in cowboy gear came up to me afterwards in tears. He said he had grown up in Truro, Cornwall and had gone to Sunday School. In those days he recalled loving the Bible stories and giving his life to Jesus. Life had gone on and he had totally forgotten about that until that night. We had the joy of leading him back to Jesus and connecting him with a local church.

Music, of different genres, has continued to inspire me down through the years, but no one has touched me quite as deeply as Johnny Cash, the "Man in Black". How about you?

* * *

53. WORRIERS OR WARRIORS?

Are you a worrier, or a warrior? If you are anything like me, you fluctuate between the two, possibly falling more into the former category if we are honest.

It comforts me a lot that Jesus in his teachings does not condemn us for this. After all, he created us and he understands our frailties. In Matthew 6 we read about Jesus teaching His followers, "Do not worry or be anxious about what you will eat or what you will wear. Do not worry about tomorrow, because tomorrow has enough cares of its own". Jesus went on to say that we should seek first his Kingdom and his righteousness and then all of these practical things would be added to us.

Many times throughout the Bible we are being encouraged not to fret; not to be afraid; not to let our hearts be troubled; not to be anxious etc. Jesus is the Prince of Peace and He came to give us peace; Jesus came to fill us full of joy; Jesus wants to fill us to overflowing with His love; and Jesus wants to give us hope and faith. Truly He is a good God.

Now that's all great and we really do need to embrace the good things that God has for us in Christ. What has been stirring in me, though, in recent days is that God has also called us to be warriors.

The Apostle Paul wrote to his young protégé Timothy and said, "Endure hard times as a good soldier of Jesus Christ". Paul also wrote to encourage us to fight the good fight of faith. In the book of Ephesians, the same writer says, "We do not wrestle (fight) against flesh and blood but we do war against spiritual forces and demons in heavenly places."

In my recent article on the subject of weapons of mass destruction, I suggested that prayer and intercession is a powerful weapon that we should be using against our common enemy, the Devil, who has come to steal, to kill and to destroy.

I truly believe that this coronavirus pandemic is Satanic and comes from the pit of Hell and its commendable to see how politicians, scientists and medics around the world are battling to find answers and deal with this the best they can. I've been asking myself, however, what should we as the Church be doing to play our part.

A great many local churches are doing a brilliant job in terms of caring for their communities through food banks, supporting the homeless, victims of domestic abuse etc. but is that all we are meant to be?

Truly I believe, God is looking for a warrior Church who will engage head on with its enemy, the Devil, and destroy this evil coronavirus with our weapons of mass destruction.

Back in Genesis 1, God said to Adam as he placed him in the centre of the Garden of Eden that he should rule and reign in the Earth, having authority over all things. Of course, when Adam and Eve sinned against God, they surrendered that authority to the Devil, but at the cross, Jesus defeated the Devil, said "It is finished" and He took back the authority from the Devil. Now by the power of the Holy Spirit living on the inside of every believer, God expects us to rule in the Earth and subdue the powers of darkness under our feet. I have a feeling that the Asian and African Church is better at this than we are in the West, but I sense it's time we rose up and took our rightful place in the Army of God. It's wrong to leave it all to the politicians, scientists and doctors. They are straining every sinew to defeat this deadly disease, but it is, I believe in the spirit realm where the victory will be won.

My heart-cry is … across the United Kingdom, let the warrior Church rise up and go to war to defeat this deadly virus once and for all.

* * *

54. YOUR MOVE!

I well remember playing scrabble, dominoes or draughts and, after a lengthy wait with no action, someone would impatiently pipe up "Your Move". I think that also happens in some card games.

A few days ago, while in prayer, I sensed the Holy Spirit saying those words to me, "It's … Your Move". I have been thinking on that since then. Since starting my Facebook posts at the start of the coronavirus lockdown, I have tried to tune in to what the Lord might be saying, not just to me, but also to share with you.

I am now convinced that God is saying "It's … Your Move" to many of us.

To those who are reading this and have read many of my other articles, you may be thinking, "I wish I could hear God, the way that John seems to", or perhaps you would just like to know God for yourself? If that's you, God is saying to you right now, "It's … Your Move".

In the Bible God says, "Draw near to me and I will draw near to you". God is a wonderful Father and He wants to have a personal relationship with you. God came to earth in the form of a baby named Jesus. Jesus lived on this planet for 33 years, doing nothing but good to people, before surrendering his life to death upon a cross to take in his own body, the wrongdoing of all mankind. Jesus rose from the dead and is alive today, seeking to have a relationship with all who will come to him.

I came to him at a church in London at the age of 21, simply thanking him for his death and resurrection and for taking my sins into his own body. On that night, I received Jesus as my Lord and he came in and gradually changed my life. In fact, he is still changing me today. He is the most wonderful friend I have. Jesus did it all on the cross and cried out "It is finished", now it's Your Move.

Perhaps you are already a Christian, but you feel dried up, disillusioned and powerless. Maybe dreams you have had in the past have not been fulfilled, a call of God upon your life that has not yet materialized, or a healing that has not yet manifested. As we come through this pandemic and lockdown restrictions are gradually lifted, I believe God is bringing us all into a new season of refreshing. The Holy Spirit has been poured out and there are rivers of his grace and power out there to flow in. God has not finished with you yet, the best is yet to be and God is saying, "It's Your Move" so come on in and fully embrace all that God has for you, with renewed hope, faith and vision.

Finally I believe God is looking for an army of believers, who full of the Holy Spirit, will be willing to go out wherever He sends them, to drive out the demonic, heal the sick and raise the dead, if necessary. It's high time for the Kingdom of God to come and his will to be done here on Earth as it is in Heaven. You have been crucified with Christ, now He lives in you and you live by the faith of the Son of God and it's Christ in you the hope of Glory. If you have not yet been filled to overflowing with the Holy Spirit, then thirst for that and you will receive all the power you need. God has poured out his Spirit freely and without measure, now "It's Your Move".

Summing up, we spend much of our lives waiting for God, when in actual fact it is God waiting for us. In many ways God has done all he is going to do. He has sent his Son to be our Saviour, poured out the Holy Spirit to give us power, and now he is saying "It's ...YOUR MOVE!".

APPENDIX

I love the songs of legendary American folk/country music singer-songwriter, John Denver. One of his most popular songs and albums was, *Poems, Prayers and Promises*. That would have been a fitting title for this Appendix in which I would like to share with you some of my favourite poems, prayers and songs which I have collected over the years...

* * *

NEW SONGS FROM AN OVERFLOWING HEART

These are a collection of words, and sometimes melodies, that have come to me as my heart has overflowed with worship to God:

The first was way back in 1970 and is to the tune of the well-known song *Show Me the Way to go Home*

You're a great and a wonderful God
You're the bread of life to me.
You're the King of Kings and the Lord of Lords
You're a great and a wonderful God.

This one was a few years later and is to the chorus of the George Formby song *Leaning on a Lamppost*

You're absolutely wonderful and marvellous and beautiful
And nobody can understand why
Jesus Christ the Son of God should die upon Calvary's cross
To save a wretched sinner such as I.

The words of the following song came to me while I was at a prayer meeting at Harvest Bible College, Redruth in 1988. One morning we were praying for the Nations, in particular Russia, and as I sang in tongues I had the distinct impression of God sending forth proclaimers to the nations of the world declaring "Jesus reigns". After singing in tongues for a while the Spirit of God urged me to sing out in English and these are the words that came.

As the Gospel is preached
Many people are reached
In every nation of the world Jesus reigns.
Across the face of the Earth
There is life and new birth
Don't you know in your heart, Jesus reigns.

He is moving every hour
By the Spirit's mighty power
Sing and dance, clap your hands, Jesus reigns.
He is Lord of every nation
He is King of all creation
So I boldly now proclaim, Jesus reigns.

He is moving in my heart
He is changing every part
I'm glad to say in me, Jesus reigns.
Send me now Lord I pray
Send me now Lord today
To the world to let them know, Jesus reigns.

A similar pattern to that above in that I was singing in tongues during a house group worship time and, when prompted by the Spirit of God to sing in English, the following words came.

I want to do something crazy
I want to do something good
I want to do something crazy for you Lord
To love you
To trust you
To depend upon your Word
I want to do something crazy for you Lord.

The following words came to me on the mornings of 15, 16 & 17 November 2003 whilst on holiday with Sylvia in Lanzarote.

There's a new song in my heart today
It's a song of praise and I shout hurray.
The battle's done, the victory's won
And Jesus Christ is the champion
I shout his name into the skies
As around the world his people rise
To acclaim their God and coming King
For Jesus reigns over everything.

There's a new song in my heart today
It's a song of joy in every way
For the King of Glory lives in me
And his reign on earth is a certainty.
So I'll hail the One who has conquered death
As day by day he gives me breath
To stand in faith and proclaim his name
Yesterday, today and forever the same.

There's a new song in my heart today
It's a song of freedom that's here to stay
For the blood of Christ has cleansed my sin
I'm a new creation, I'm born again.
By his stripes I have been healed
And the lies of Satan have been revealed
With Christ in me it's a brand-new story
Every breath I have is to give Him glory.

These words and a tune came to me whilst I was walking into Solihull on the morning of 21 October 2008 just two days after the death of my dear Father.

I want to sing my praise to you
I want to sing my praise to you
I want to tell the world how great you are

I want to sing my praise to you.

My heart is full of joy
My heart is full of joy
I want to tell the world how great you are
Because my heart is full of joy.

I want to dance before you Lord
I want to dance before you Lord
To celebrate and bring you joy
I want to dance before you Lord.

The words and tune of this little ditty came to me walking back from Solihull on the morning of Saturday 8 November 2008.

Lord you're so magnificent, yes you are
Lord you're so amazing, yes you are
Lord you're so incredible, so wise and so true
And there's nothing impossible for you
No there's nothing too hard
And there's nothing too difficult for you.

These words and melody came to me in my kitchen one Saturday morning in 2015 a few days before I was to have a biopsy on my prostate.

This is my song of deliverance
This is my song of praise
And that is why to you my God
My hands I now do raise.

These words came to me in March 2017 whilst caring for Sylvia.

Never say never again
No never say never again
With God all things are possible
So never say never again.

Ask and you will receive
Seek and you will find
Knock and the door will be opened to you
So never say never again

Song in My Heart (18 August 2017)

I have woken up this morning with a song I want to sing
It's one of praise to Jesus, my Lord, my God, my King.
He's brought me through so many things, I don't know where to start
So I'll just begin to thank him, as I open up my heart.

Thank you for the fire that burns within my heart each day
To tell the world of your great love as I journey on my way.
Your presence is so real, your kindness so immense
I pray that all will turn to you and see your relevance.

I want to sing and shout, to praise you all day long
For in my heart their lives this great salvation song.
It bubbles up and overflows
Until every nation knows
That Jesus Christ reigns with arms unfurled
As the Saviour and champion of the world.

On Thursday morning of 5 December 2019, I was singing in tongues when I sensed the Holy Spirit saying, "Sing me a simple song" and then these words came to me.

A simple song I bring
A simple song I sing
A simple song of worship to Jesus Christ my King.
Hallelujah! Hallelujah!
To Jesus Christ my King.

* * *

A SELECTION OF INSPIRING POEMS, PRAYERS AND HYMNS

WORKPLACE PRAYER

My Heavenly Father, as I enter this workplace, I bring Your presence with me. I speak Your peace, Your grace, Your mercy, and Your perfect order into this office. I acknowledge Your power over all that will be spoken, thought, decided, and done within these walls.

Lord, I thank You for the gifts you have blessed me with. I commit to using them responsibly in Your honour. Give me a fresh supply of strength to do my job. Anoint my projects, ideas, and energy, so that even my smallest accomplishment may bring You glory. Lord, when I am confused, guide me. When I am weary, energize me. When I am burned out, infuse me with the light of the Holy Spirit. May the work that I do and the way I do it bring faith, joy, and a smile to all that I come in contact with today.

And oh Lord, when I leave this place, give me travelling mercy. Bless my family and home to be in order as I left it. Lord, I thank you for everything You've done, everything You're doing, and everything You're going to do.

In the Name of Jesus, I pray, with much love and thanksgiving ... Amen

THE SCOPE OF PRAYER (ANON)

Through prayer there is no problem that can't be solved,
no sickness that can't be healed,
no burden that can't be lifted,
no storm that can't be weathered,
no devastation that can't be relieved,
no sorrow that can't be erased,
no poverty cycle that can't be broken,
no sinner that can't be saved,

no perishing that can't be rescued,
no fallen that can't be lifted,
no hurt that can't be removed,
no broken relationship that can't be mended,
no difference that can't be resolved,
no hindrance that can't be shaken,
no limitation that can't be overcome,
no mourning that can't be comforted,
no ashes that can't become beauty,
no heaviness that can't be covered with the garment of praise,
no thirst that can't be quenched, no hunger that can't be filled,
no dry ground that can't be flooded,
no desert that can't blossom,
no congregation that can't be revived,
no preacher that can't be anointed,
no church pews that can't be filled,
no nation that can't be transformed.

A HEART LIKE THINE *Source: The Song Book of the Salvation Army*

I want, dear Lord, a heart that's true and clean,
A sunlit heart, with not a cloud between;
A heart like thine, a heart divine,
A heart as white as snow;
On me, dear Lord, a heart like this bestow.

I want, dear Lord, a love that cares for all,
A deep, strong love that answers every call;
A love like thine, a love divine,
A love to come or go;
On me, dear Lord, a love like this bestow.

I want, dear Lord, a soul on fire for thee,
A soul baptised with heavenly energy;
A willing mind, a ready hand
To do whate'er I know,
To spread thy light wherever I may go.

DISTURB US, O LORD

Sir Francis Drake (1540 - 1596) was the first Englishman to circumnavigate the globe. In 1581 he was knighted by Queen Elizabeth I for his accomplishment. This poem, which is attributed to him, inspires and challenges us to dream big, to sail out beyond the safety of the shore, and live boldly for God.

Disturb us, O Lord,
When we are too pleased with ourselves,
When our dreams have come true
Because we dreamed too little,
When we arrived safely
Because we sailed too close to the shore.
Disturb us, O Lord,
When with the abundance of things we possess
We have lost our thirst for the waters of life;
Having fallen in love with life,
We have ceased to dream of eternity
And in our efforts to build a new earth,
We have allowed our vision of the new Heaven to dim.
Disturb us, O Lord,
To dare more boldly,
To venture on wilder seas,
Where storms will show Your mastery;
Where losing sight of land,
We shall find the stars.
We ask you to push back
The horizons of our hopes;
And to push back the future
In strength, courage, hope, and love.
This we ask in the name of our Captain,
Who is Jesus Christ.

FLOODS OF REVIVAL (Sung to the tune of Blessed Assurance)

Floods of revival Lord let them fall.

Streams of salvation reaching to all.
Pour out thy spirit, great is our need.
Sweep o'er our beings, now whilst we plead.

Spirit divine, O, quicken us now,
Whilst in thy presence humbly we bow.
Set all our hearts ablaze with thy love,
teach us the secret of life from above.

Utterly yielded, longing to know
all the blest fullness love can bestow.
Ready and willing eager to give
perfect obedience, bravely to live.

Raise up a people holy and free;
hearts with a vision like unto thee.
Souls that would rather die than give in;
Lives with a passion, victory to win.

O for a deluge of Holy Ghost power,
Lord we are waiting send it this hour.
Open the windows of heaven we pray.
All on the altar gladly we lay.

TO GIVE AND NOT TO COUNT THE COST (Saint Ignatius of Loyola)

Teach us, good Lord,
to serve you as you deserve,
to give and not to count the cost,
to fight and not to heed the wounds,
to toil and not to seek for rest,
to labour and not to ask for any reward,
save that of knowing that we do your will.

Amen.

I RISE TODAY (St Patrick's Prayer)

I bind unto myself today the power of God to hold and lead, his eye to watch, his might to stay, his ear to harken to my need, the wisdom of my God to teach,

his hand to guide, his shield to ward, the Word of God to give me speech, his heavenly host to be my guard. Christ be with me, Christ within me, Christ

behind me, Christ before me, Christ beside me, Christ to win me; Christ to comfort and restore me; Christ beneath me, Christ above me, Christ in quiet,

Christ in danger, Christ in hearts of all that love me, Christ in mouth of friend and stranger. I bind unto myself the name, the strong name of the Trinity,

by invocation of the same, the Three in One, and One in Three, of whom all nature hath creation, eternal Father, Spirit, Word; praise to the God of my

salvation, salvation is of Christ the Lord!

QUOTE FROM RALPH WALDO EMERSON

"You cannot do a kindness too soon, for you never know how soon it will be too late."

* * *

PRAYERS FROM THE HEART
- gathered by me, over the years, from a whole variety of places.

Lord of life, help me to demonstrate in my daily life something of the courage and strength of the character of Jesus. I want to be someone who takes a stand against injustice and the abuse of power. Help me to do this, I pray, with wisdom, discernment and boldness. Amen.

O Lord, help me to outmanoeuvre any sinful thoughts that come into my mind. Give me the kind of mind in which You can be at home. This I ask in Jesus' peerless and precious name. Amen.

O Father, my appetite is being whetted. Help me "launch out into the deep" and give myself to You in the way that You are willing to give Yourself to me. In Christ's name I ask it. Amen.

O Father, the thought that I, a sinner saved by grace, am able to send Satan into retreat almost overwhelms me. Yet I must believe it, for Your Word tells me so. Help me understand even more clearly the authority I have in Christ. In His name I ask it. Amen.

Lord, help me to travel light, and when I discern the temptation to wickedness in myself, give me the grace to overcome it so that I may be a blessing to all I meet and bring joy to your heart. Amen.

Lord, I wonder, am I thirsty or desperate enough to make this matter of being filled with the Spirit my top priority? Help me to face up to the challenge now. For Jesus' sake. Amen.

Heavenly Father, I thank you for my body. It is a great place to live in when things are going okay; be with me when things go wrong. Help me not to take my body for granted and help me look after it. Amen.

O God, You who are always reaching out to me in generosity and love, help me this day to do the same. May You use my generosity to touch the lives of others. For Your own dear name's sake. Amen.

O Father, forgive me for the times I rush into Your presence intent only on getting my needs met. Slow me down and make me a more contemplative person. Then Your character can rub off on mine. In Jesus' name I pray. Amen.

Dear Heavenly Father, whose dear Son was bullied, I pray for all bullies: those who bully at work, in school or college, and those leaders of nations who use their country to bully others. Help me to find a way of living in peace with others with mutual respect, care and concern. Amen.

Lord, help me to remember that I am one of your ambassadors to those around me. Help me not to be entangled by the evil that surrounds me, but to live in the power of your resurrection, as I seek your mind for the message I need to proclaim to this needy world. Amen.

Lord, I confess that in the past I have lived a life that has displeased you. Even when I have tried to please you, I have often failed because of my ignorance and pride. I pray that the risen Christ would once again take centre stage in my life. Amen.

Father, what a rich heritage you have given me! Thank you for my Father Abraham who just believed you and everything changed. I decide to walk into this day standing tall in my heritage and knowing that the only opinion of me that matters says: "Right with God". I praise you! Amen.

O Father, help me to be an honest person. Help me to absorb Your love in such a measure that it will dissolve every fear. Then strengthen me to face life, fearless and unafraid. Amen.

Father, Son, and Holy Spirit, though I cannot comprehend Your essential oneness and unity, I can worship You nevertheless. This I do now, in humble adoration. Glory, honour, and power be unto Your name forever and ever. Amen.

O Father, take me from life limited to Life Unlimited. I have lived far too long in the nest. Now I want to get up into the air. Amen.

Thank you for reminding me today that you are looking for me not only to hear you but to obey you. It's exciting to know that when Jonah eventually obeyed, a whole nation was saved. Help me to hear, obey and see significant things happen in me and through me. Amen.

Lord, I pray that you will come and wake me up with your kiss of love. I don't want to remain asleep, comfortable and ineffective. Lord, I want to have a deep passion in my heart for Jesus and see lives changed by the power of God. Amen.

Lord, thank you that you love me so much. Help me to know and to understand that love more and more. Please expose anything hidden within me and set me free from anything that would keep me in bondage and lead me away from you. Change me from within – make me more like Jesus. Amen.

Lord, thank you that you can use ordinary people like me to affect a nation. Lord, I want to see my nation profoundly changed by the power of God. Help me to hear, obey and trust you in every area of my life and expect miracles to happen. Amen.

O yes, dear Father, from the depths of my being I cry out, "Make me clean". I have come so far with You - how can I turn back now? I'm a candidate for both power and purity. Give me the deep inner cleansing I need - today. For Jesus' sake. Amen.

Loving Father, I pray for all those who are having a really hard time at the moment. May they be particularly aware of your love and protection. Give them the faith to hold onto you, come what may. In Jesus' name, Amen.

Search me, O God, and know my heart; test me and know my thoughts. Point out anything in me that offends you and lead me along the path of everlasting life. Amen.

Heavenly Father, I thank you for the blessings and the victories that are coming my way, but while I am waiting for them, please help me to celebrate the blessings that you give others. In Jesus' name, Amen.

Heavenly Father, thank you that you place people in my life to give me good advice. Forgive me if I have been too proud to take advice in the past and help me to follow good advice in the future, that I might benefit others as well as myself. In Jesus' name, Amen.

O Father, teach me how to turn the ugly into the beautiful, the evil into the good, and take every project prisoner for Christ. I ask this for Your own dear name's sake. Amen.

Help me to trust you Lord. It isn't easy when all around me often seems muddled and difficult.
Help me to listen for your call, Lord, for I want to serve you.
I bring before you the needs of your aching world.
I bring before you the joys of your beautiful world.
I bring before you the concerns of my heart this day.
May fairness and justice, patience and understanding be in all my actions and decisions.
Grant me the grace to forgive and love others as you forgive and love me.
Amen.

Dear God, Please help me live my life in front of people with honesty and integrity. I don't have anything to hide. I want to be transparent so that people can see Jesus through me. Amen.

Lord God, I want to let you in to deal with these enemies of yours in me. I need you to set me free from the stuff that chokes the growth of your kingdom in me. Presumably it won't be easy but, even to get to this point, is a bit of a miracle. I'm going to praise and thank you, Lord God, and celebrate your victory in style! Amen.

Dear God, when our days are disrupted, when we face upheavals and when things don't go the way we had planned, give us eyes to see your hand at work and strength to believe that you are in charge and are gently shepherding us with your love. In Jesus name, Amen.

Lord God, forgive me when I am impatient, or too easily give up. Forgive me when I am too cautious, or unwilling to step out in faith with You. Please give me grace sufficient that I might be persistent in prayer, willing to take risks with You and to serve You courageously all the days of my life. Amen.

Lord God, I want to become more like Jesus Christ, to be turned on by the things that please you and turned off by the things that offend you. Show me your mind so that I will see you more clearly, love you more dearly, and follow you more nearly, day by day. Amen.

Father God, deliver me from the deadness of 'other things.' Saturate me with the oil of your Spirit that I may be a flame. Make me your fuel, flame of God. Amen.

Father, I want to act in love, not react in anger. Instead of being short-tempered and striking back, help me to be patient and turn the other cheek. Today let Your love rule my life, for Christ's sake, Amen.

Father, protector, help me watch my mouth, mind and heart today. Please show to me areas where I've been slipping up and help me to overcome them. Help me love and follow You today. Amen.

Father, healer, we're all broken people. Please help me see where I need to be changed and guide me through that. Please come and help me live for and love You today. Amen.

Lord Jesus, take away all my fears and anything in my life that could cause me to sin. Give me the strength to not take the easy option out when times are hard and the world is against You. I pray that I will have the courage to witness for You even when I'm under pressure. Help me to make sure that my words and actions do not deny You as the King of my heart and life. Amen.

Lord, everything seems to be falling apart around me. Everybody wants a piece of me. There's far too much to do and never enough time to do it. My head is clogged with all kinds of junk and my heart is ready to break. Lord, where are You? I feel like the disciples in the storm, the waves are too big for me. My cry is the same as theirs, "Somebody go and get Jesus - I'm about to drown out here! Prince of Peace I need you. Amen.

Father, who never slumbers nor sleeps, take charge. Let me find in You a quiet place, a place where I can rest my head on Your breast, hear Your loving heartbeat and feel secure knowing You'll work things out for me. This I pray, believing, in Jesus' name, Amen.

Father, even when I feel dry and desolate, your Word and your Spirit bring me new life and hope. I offer you my "dry bones" for renewal and transformation. Amen.

Father, Your Word says that You are "the only wise God" and I am desperately in need of You at this time. I'm in a situation human wisdom can't explain and human ability can't fix. There's only one way out - that's through You! Send the spirit of wisdom and show me which way to go. Send the spirit of revelation to help me understand what I can't figure out, for nobody but You can get me through this. Help me to faithfully obey all You show me to do, and to remember that sometimes the wisdom of this world is foolishness to You. Help me to know the difference between human advice and godly advice, and to choose Your way. I submit this situation to You and commit myself to following You, knowing You've promised to direct my steps. Help me to walk this road with confidence in You; with the courage that comes from knowing I am Yours. Help me to cling to my convictions, yet still love those who misunderstand me. Keep me far from anger and close to Your heart. And though it's an uphill climb, take my hand, light my way and help me to walk on, for in the end I know that all things will work together for my good and Your glory: in Christ's name. Amen.

Father, help me to reject all thoughts of scarcity. Show me how to help others achieve their goals by sharing my time, talents and treasure. In Jesus' name, I pray. Amen.

Father thank You for the relationships You've blessed me with. I make a decision today to release anyone who has ever offended me in the slightest…to overlook it… forget about it, and move on. I will not keep a record of their wrongs. I will offer mercy and unconditional love. In Jesus' name. Amen

Lord Jesus, You are our Saviour, taking all the sin, hatred, illness and death to the cross, rising from the grave, victorious over all the earth. We receive your healing, believing that your power carries ultimate authority. We leave this illness at the cross and walk freely healed and restored by Your amazing grace. Amen.

Father, it feels like I'm in an impossible position with no way out. Let me feel Your presence and the encouragement of Your Spirit, reminding me that with You all things are possible to those who believe. Send the answer from heaven to my earthly situation. From where I stand, things look hopeless. But You are the God who created the earth from nothing and rolled back the Red Sea so Your children could cross over safely. You made the blind to see, the lame to walk, and the deaf to hear. Today I thank You that You're my God, and that You are "always ready to help in times of trouble." Amen.

Father, Let the fire of your Holy presence fill my being today so that I may walk in the power of Jesus Christ my Lord. I ask this in Jesus' name and for your glory. Amen.

Breathe on Me, Breath of God

Breathe on me, Breath of God,
Fill me with life anew,
That I may love what Thou dost love,
And do what Thou wouldst do.

Breathe on me, Breath of God,
Until my heart is pure,
Until with Thee I will one will,
To do and to endure.

Breathe on me, Breath of God,
Till I am wholly Thine,
Until this earthly part of me
Glows with Thy fire divine.

Breathe on me, Breath of God,
So shall I never die,
But live with Thee the perfect life
Of Thine eternity.

Edwin Hatch 1878

ACKNOWLEDGEMENTS

Thanks to all my family for the way you have supported me through the coronavirus lockdown.

Thanks to Allan and Diane Davis and Malcolm and Wendy Beamond for your daily encouragement and prayers.

Thanks to you, my Facebook friends for your kind comments and encouragement to publish this book for the benefit of a wider readership.

Thanks to Elizabeth Webb for, not only proofreading and 'being my eyes' for the production of this book, but for your ceaseless encouragement over many years. You set me this challenge and I hope I have done you proud.

Finally, and most importantly…

Thanks to God my loving Father, to Jesus Christ my Lord and Saviour and to the Holy Spirit, my guide, my guard and my friend.

From my Grateful Heart to Yours,

John

email: john@flanner.co.uk

website: www.johnflanner.co.uk

Other books by the same author ...

Available from:

email: john@flanner.co.uk

or order from all good bookstores

FEAR, FUN and FAITH

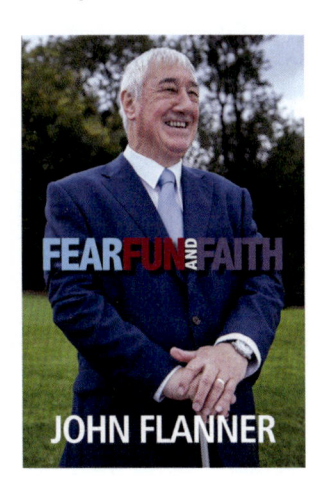

John Flanner was a typical football-mad teenager until, at the age of 19, he was robbed of his sight to a rare hereditary condition. As a shy, self-deprecating young man growing up in 1960s Birmingham, John was already battling many fears and phobias before his subsequent blindness plunged him into a world of darkness.

However, John's determination to succeed, faith in God and the ability to see the potential in every situation led to the rise of a Brummie-born man who conquered his fears. John was the first recipient of the prestigious National Civil Service Diversity Award in 2006 becoming a sought-after motivational speaker using his personal experiences in overcoming unexpected disability to inspire and encourage businessmen and women across the UK.

Fear Fun and Faith is the inspirational story of an ordinary man who has led an extraordinary life. Join John as he takes you through the twists and turns of his personal journey with his trademark humour and witty writing style, peppered with plenty of emotional anecdotes and more than one miracle along the way.

ISBN 978-0-9934175-0-4

Available for order from john@flanner.co.uk and all good bookstores.

BITZARO TO BUCKINGHAM

Acclaimed writer John Flanner is back with the second instalment of his autobiography that takes us from Bitzaro Palace on the Greek shores all the way back to Buckingham Palace on home soil. Starting with a series of traumatic events on holiday resulting in an air ambulance ride back to England, John's story unfolds as he finds himself caring for his wife while facing new challenges in his working career.

The events on that fateful holiday and John's unswerving faith and fervour both personally and professionally, led to him receiving one of the highest accolades, an honour from Her Majesty the Queen. Displaying his heart and his humour in the pages, John's wonderful writing style captivates the reader who will likely experience an equal measure of laughter and tears as he takes them on a journey through the last ten years of his life.

Being focused on the encouragement and empowerment of others on their own journey whilst overcoming personal illness and obstacles, John's inspirational story shows how one man has defied the odds and continues to reach new heights as he follows God's path for his life.

ISBN 978-0-9934175-2-8

Available for order from john@flanner.co.uk and all good bookstores.

BEAUTIFUL GAME BEAUTIFUL MEMORIES

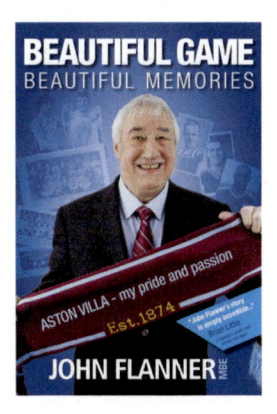

John Flanner scores his very own hat trick with his third book that takes football fans on a trip down memory lane. A self-confessed super-supporter, John pays homage to the 'Beautiful Game', and the many memories he has amassed over the years while following his treasured club Aston Villa FC.

As you read John's vivid accounts of legendary matches from the 1950s to the present day, you will find yourself transported to the very stadiums where the dramatic events of a bygone era unfolded. You can sense the electric atmosphere, hear the booming chants and experience the edge of your seat excitement as John recalls the magical moments when football heroes past and present made footballing history.

From the pain of relegation and multiple management changes to the euphoria of being European Champions, John takes the reader on a journey through the last half century of league and cup football. John shares his passion for his beloved sport alongside many amusing anecdotes, in his usual compelling style. This book is a must-read for any sport enthusiast who shares John's love of football... so sit back and enjoy reliving the beautiful memories through the blind eyes of a fervent football supporter.

ISBN 978-0-9934175-5-9

Available for order from john@flanner.co.uk and all good bookstores.